Writing for 100 Days

A Student-Centered Approach to Composition and Creative Writing

Gabriel Arquilevich, M.F.A.

Fairview Publishing
Ventura County, California

Requests for permission and for orders should be mailed to the following address: Fairview Publishing, P.O. Box 746, Oak View, CA 93022

Printed in the United States of America

ISBN: 0-9649042-0-9

Writing for 100 Days

A Student-Centered Approach to Composition and Creative Writing

ACKNOWLEDGMENTS

For their help in reviewing and editing the manuscript I thank David Howard and Mary Embree. For their ongoing encouragement and support I am grateful to Bonnie and Lawrence Williams. Thank you to Ron Arquilevich for his help designing the cover of the book. I thank my wife and friend, Jaymie Arquilevich, for her patience, her love and her support.

This book is dedicated to my students, who have taught me the value of teaching.

ABOUT THE AUTHOR

Gabriel Arquilevich holds a B.A. in English from Johnston College and an M.F.A. in Poetry from the University of Massachusetts in Amherst. In addition to his six years of teaching experience, he is the author of several educational publications, including *World Religions* (Teacher Created Materials), and the complete high school literature curricula for Oak Meadow School, an international home schooling center based in Blacksburg, VA. Currently, in addition to his work as a freelance writer, Mr. Arquilevich teaches English at Oak Grove School, in Ojai, CA.

Introduction to Teachers

An uninspired curriculum is dangerous to students. This is especially true when it comes to writing. Unfortunately, many of us learn how to write by memorizing grammar rules, diagramming sentences, and completing countless exercises. Although these activities are beneficial, *they don't teach a student how to write!* If you want to learn how to fly a kite, you get a few pointers, and then you *try it;* in other words, the best teacher of writing is *writing!* But when students follow a textbook from cover to cover, when they write in isolation and relate writing to participial phrases and predicate nominatives, they are in danger. Thankfully, educators are recognizing the need for change. This book answers that need by providing a fresh approach to writing instruction.

Here are some of the features that make *Writing for 100 Days* unique:

- The text is written with the student in mind. This translates into a friendly tone and a sensitivity to the questions and difficulties a student is likely to have. Therefore, the question, "How does this apply to writing?" appears in many lessons.

- It is a *comprehensive* approach. In addition to practicing composition, fiction, and poetry, students write letters, articles, speeches, manuals, and even greeting cards. Thus, they discover how their writing skills are used in the real world.

- It is a *manageable* approach. English textbooks are intimidating, especially when they include all areas of the subject. The content and feel of *100 Days* encourages students and teachers to focus solely on the process of writing.

- Many of the assignments are group-oriented, providing an alternative to the traditional student/teacher exchange. Working together, students are exposed to a variety of writing styles while sharpening their critical eye. This releases the student and teacher from the isolation of classroom writing.

- Every lesson includes a writing activity that brings the learning into application. These activities last from 1-5 days. (A list of additional writing assignments appears in the back of the book.) Exercises are kept to a minimum.

- In order to learn, students are asked to *make mistakes.* For example, after reading about clichés, they write a story using plenty of overused expressions. This strategy helps students recognize their own errors more easily. It's also more fun than memorizing grammar rules. Afterwards, they rewrite one another's stories, making the necessary corrections.

A Note on the Structure

As the title suggests, the text provides students with writing activities for 100 days. These days are divided into four sections: composition, fiction, poetry, and "writing in action." Let's take a look at the features of each.

Composition: A step beyond the rudimentary rules of usage and punctuation, these **forty-eight days** focus on word choice, sentence structure, grammar, style, and more. *A variety of related (and original!) exercises and writing activities help bring the learning into application.* Included is a look at dashes, parentheses, colons and semicolons.

Note: The book begins with the assumption that the basic parts of speech and rudimentary punctuation have been learned. Nouns, verbs, commas, and end marks should be reviewed as needed.

Fiction: Beginning with character development, students lay the groundwork for a story in **fifteen days.** Studies of dialogue and point of view are provided.

Poetry: In these **ten days**, students practice a variety of forms, from sonnets to song lyrics. Also included is a look at imagery and line break.

Writing in Action: These **twenty-seven** days introduce to the student a variety of nonfiction forms, including letter writing, speech writing, technical writing, journalism, and advertising. This section also presents some unusual writing tasks, including an epistolary, a fictitious diary, and "fun and games" activities.

Note: The four fingers signify a new day's assignment. They look like this:

☞   ☞   ☞   ☞

How to Use *Writing for 100 Days*

Although *Writing for 100 Days* is carefully structured, it is meant to be flexible. The effectiveness of the process, therefore, depends greatly on the sensitivity of the teacher. This cannot be overemphasized.

For example, if students are enjoying (or struggling with) a one-day assignment, *give them another day.* Keep in mind that most of the assignments are allotted the minimum amount of days necessary for their completion.

Likewise, you should move from section to section when it's appropriate. If a student is weary of composition, for instance, try some poetry or a word game.

Here are a few teaching tips to keep in mind as you go through the lessons:

- Review the book before beginning. This will let the students know what to expect in the coming days. Allow time for feedback and questions.

- Have students keep a portfolio of their writing. This will help you determine a final grade; it will also give the students a sense of accomplishment.

- Whenever you sense the class is in a "writing rut," have a change of pace. A stream-of-consciousness piece is always an excellent alternative.

- Expose students to different types of writing in the real world. If they're writing a travel article, for example, feature a few articles on the bulletin board.

- Overhead transparencies are excellent tools for teaching writing. They allow the class to look at a piece together, whether it be a published model or a student's work.

- Supplement the course with literature. Use excerpts to demonstrate writing strategies or poetic forms.

- Invite guest writers to visit the classroom. It makes a difference to students when they can meet a real journalist, poet, or novelist.

- Given the emphasis on group learning, create a classroom setting that encourages students to work *together.*   Here are a few suggestions:

  a) Pay special attention to the opening lesson, "Before Beginning: Writing About Writing." This lesson includes an open discussion about writing: What are their feelings? Is writing a hardship? What are the most challenging aspects of writing? What's their favorite kind of writing? How do they think they learn best? How is writing used in the "real world"?

     This kind of exchange is extremely beneficial in any classroom. By letting the students know that you're sensitive to their needs, you establish trust. They should be able to say when they're struggling.

  b) Set up a bulletin board that features student writing. Create themes that reflect the assignments and decorate the board accordingly. Include published pieces as well.

  c) Be sure that the classroom is set up to accommodate group learning. You might want the desks in a circle; you might want to provide a sofa.

A Word for Home Schoolers

The tone and style of the book lend themselves very well to home schooling. In fact, it's likely that a disciplined 8th-12th grader could go through the book without the constant guidance of a teacher. Certainly, the process is not dependent on a classroom, although some of the group assignments will need to be adjusted to fit a home schooling environment.

Keep in mind that the book emphasizes interaction. You might want to partner up with another home schooling family, or do the lessons along with the student. Finally, if you don't feel confident about your own writing skills, hire a tutor who can provide feedback on some of the assignments.

Table of Contents

IV. WRITING IN ACTION

Composition

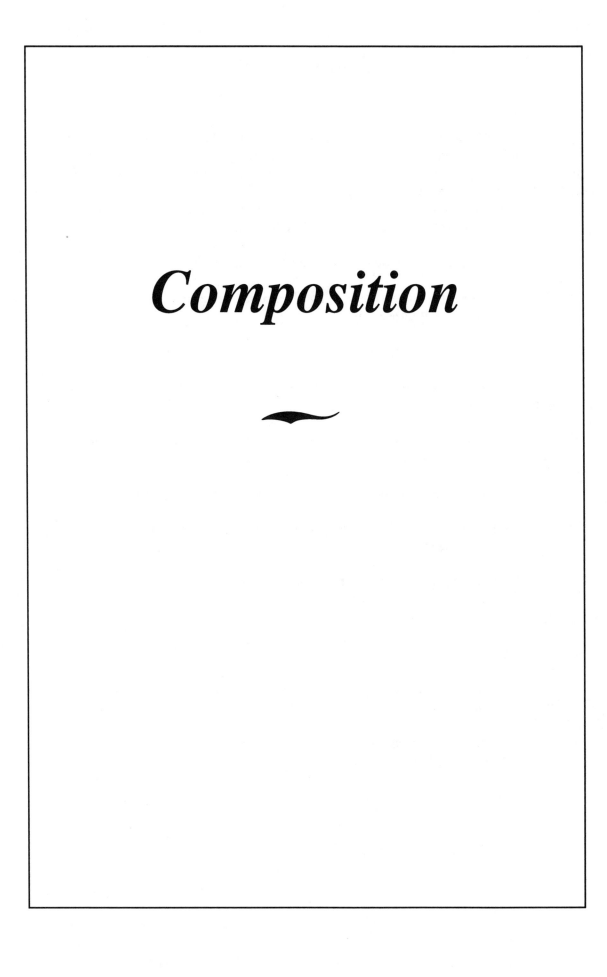

Before You Begin:
Writing About Writing

For some people, writing is a difficult task. To others, writing is a hobby, a profession, or an art. It would be worthwhile, then, for you to express your feelings about writing before beginning *Writing for 100 Days*. After all, your attitude towards writing will, to a large degree, determine the quality of work you produce.

Take 20-30 minutes to write about writing. Afterwards, share your feelings with your classmates. You might want to consider the following questions:

- What are your general feelings about writing? Do you enjoy it? Do you dislike it?

- What's the most difficult part of writing? Beginning an assignment? Spelling? Grammar? Having enough to say?

- What's most enjoyable about writing?

- Compare the writing you've done in the classroom to the writing you've done outside of school.

- How did you learn to write? Describe some of your early writing experiences. Were they positive or negative?

- What type of writing do you like the most? Which do you like the least?

- What's your most memorable writing experience? Was it a story? Was it a letter or a poem to a friend?

- If you were a writing teacher, what approach would you use? What would be the most effective way to teach writing?

A Dialogue About Writing

Now share your thoughts with your classmates. You'll find that many of you have the same anxieties about writing. These feelings are important.

Remember, you have the freedom to adjust assignments, as long as you discuss changes with your teacher. After all, it's *your* education.

Word Choice:
The Antidote to Vocabulary

Students often think they need to build an enormous vocabulary to write well or to sound sophisticated. Although an expansive vocabulary is a plus, far more important is your ability to choose the right words. Most often, the word you're looking for is *already in your vocabulary*. Take the following example:

- If you're working in the sun all day, jump in the pool. It's great.

Is there a better word than *great* to describe how it feels to cool off in a pool? What about replacing *great* with *refreshing*? Isn't *refreshing* a more appropriate word? Sometimes, one precise word can replace an entire phrase:

- She felt no one was paying any attention to her.
- She felt ignored.

Not only does attention to word choice produce more precise writing, but it also adds flavor by eliminating redundancy. If you're writing a story about a poodle, for example, and you've already said 'poodle' and 'dog' thirteen times in one page, what do you do? How about describing the dog in a new way?

-The poodle barked proudly. The curly canine was afraid of no one!

Of course, you don't want to overdo it. If you write a different description every time you mention the dog, the story would be unreadable.

One way to improve your word choice is to use the thesaurus. This reference book will give you word alternatives. However, *never use a word you're not totally comfortable with.* Don't change,

-Mr. Jones gets angry when the newspaper is not delivered.
to
-Mr. Jones gets antipathetic when the periodical is not dispatched.

Unless you're going for humor, the second sentence is a mess. So, always stay with words you know well. There are plenty of them available. The trick is wanting to find them!

Exercise

A) Rewrite the following paragraph. Replace the inexact words with precise ones; eliminate redundancy by adding new descriptions. Feel free to use a thesaurus for reference.

My first trip to the amusement park was lots of fun. The rides were exciting and terrific. There were a lot of rides, including roller coasters and other rides that were scary. At first, I didn't want to go on the scariest one. People's faces looked so scared when they went down the hills. Finally, I decided to go on the biggest roller coaster. I was so scared! Most of the time I kept my eyes closed. We went really fast and did lots of turns. When the ride was over I was glad to be back. It was scary but fun.

☞   ☞   ☞   ☞

Be a Wordsmith:
Word Choice in Action

"Wordsmith" is informal for "editor." A wordsmith's job is to hunt down bad language. Now it's your turn to fine-tune your editing skills by becoming a friend's wordsmith.

This assignment has two parts and requires a partner. First, each person writes a long paragraph describing his or her favorite movie. The compositions should be full of inexact words and redundancy.

Afterwards, exchange papers and go to work! Rewrite your partner's description, making it sparkle with newness.

Extension

Invite a professional editor to your classroom. Before he or she arrives, brainstorm a list of questions about editing.

Wordiness & Word Economy

Have you ever been offered a "free gift?" Have you ever read about "past history" in a textbook?

Aren't all gifts free? Isn't all history in the past? As you can see, both expressions are examples of *overdone phrases,* or *wordiness.* Wordiness can come in many forms, including redundancy, overdone phrases and empty expressions. Regardless, it's an enemy of good writing. Using too many words is like adding water to soda—it dilutes the flavor. A well-written sentence should contain no unnecessary words, just as a well-written paragraph should contain no unnecessary sentences. Thus, we have one of the cardinal rules for writing: *omit all unnecessary words or phrases.* This is called *word economy.*

Exercise

A) Let's begin by taking a look at a list of overdone phrases. On a separate sheet of paper, write down the corrections for each. For example, "an unexpected surprise" is simply "a surprise."

at the present time	past history	thought to myself
due to the fact	climb up	the honest truth
end result	red in color	usual custom
large in size	refer back	repeat again

You're probably familiar with most of these phrases; many of them are common to spoken English. In writing, however, such phrases are deadly. Every one of them is redundant. Of course, you may *want* to use an overdone phrase, especially in dialogue. The key is to be able to recognize them and then to decide on their use.

Empty Expressions

Empty expressions are less obvious than overdone phrases. They consist of words that add little to the meaning of a sentence. Here are some examples:

due to	it seems to me	the fact that
I think/feel	no doubt but that	the reason that
in my opinion	on account of	there is/was/are
there seems to be	resulting from	what I mean is
in order to	with regard to	the thing is

Exercise

B) The following paragraphs contain plenty of overdone phrases and empty expressions. (Not all of them appear on the lists.) Economize the language by omitting unnecessary words and phrases.

A doctor by profession, Dr. Buckwalter received an unexpected surprise when his neighbor, Mrs. Smithers, brought her sick dog into his office. Due to the fact that he had patients waiting in the waiting room, he asked Mrs. Smithers to postpone her visit until later. Mrs. Smithers started a ruckus! The end result was that Dr. Buckwalter attended to Mrs. Smithers' dog. All in all, it was an uncommonly strange situation!

At the present time, I am not going to buy the restaurant. There seem to be too many questions as to whether it will be successful or not. In the event that the restaurant did poorly, I would lose all my savings that I've saved up over the years. To tell you the honest truth, I'm not sure I'd like that to occur. So, with all due respect, I'd like to thank you for your most kind offer.

Wordiness: Essay & Revision

One fun way to learn how to avoid wordiness is by being wordy! By deliberately using overdone phrases and empty expressions, you can recognize them more easily when they creep into your writing.

This is a two-part assignment that will require a partner. First, write a half-page description of an event that took place in the past week. Add lots of wordiness to the first draft. Now read it aloud to someone. You'll probably get plenty of laughs!

Next, exchange your paper with your partner's. Rewrite each other's descriptions, eliminating unnecessary words and phrases. How much shorter did your piece become?

Prefixes, Roots, and Suffixes

Good writing is made up of words that are expressive and concise. One way to improve your word choice is to be familiar with prefixes, roots, and suffixes. Let's begin by looking at a word that contains a prefix, root, and suffix.

UN•REASON•ABLE

In this example, *reason* is the root word. The root word carries the primary meaning. *Reason* means "basis for action" or "with good sense." The prefix *un* is added **before** the root word to change or modify the meaning. *Un* means "not." The suffix *able* is added **after** the root word to change the meaning. *Able* means "sufficient ability" or "worthy of."

So, *unreasonable* can be broken down to mean "not worthy of good sense or cause for action." Of course, this is a rather awkward way of putting it! It's much better to say "unreasonable." (Notice that the word *reason* is a noun; adding the prefix and suffix make it an adjective.)

Here is a list of common prefixes and suffixes along with their meanings. Before continuing to the exercise, take a minute to study the list.

Prefix

anti—opposite, against
com, con—with, together
de—reverse, remove, undo
dis—lack of, not
extra—beyond, outside of
in—in, inside, within
inter—between, among
mis—bad, wrongly
post—after
pre—before, prior to
re—again
sub—under, subordinate
trans—across, change
un—not, reversal

Suffix

able, ible—sufficient ability, worthy of
ance, ence—state of
ant—performing, causing an action
er—one who, one that
ful—full of, abundant
ic—relating to, like
ing—performing an action
ion—a process, state of being
ite—resident of
ism—practice or process, state of
      being
ity—state of
less—lack, without
ness—condition

Exercise

A) Now it's your turn to create words using prefixes and suffixes. Drawing from the list above, make your own list of words. Be sure to use *every* prefix and suffix. Try to use both in one word. *Indestructible,* for example, has a prefix and a suffix. Save the list when you're done.

Note: Be careful not to invent words. Not all words can accommodate prefixes or suffixes. *Distruthfulness,* for instance, is not a word.

☞   ☞   ☞   ☞

Taking a Journey:
Prefixes & Suffixes in Action

Now it's time to put into practice what you've learned about prefixes and suffixes. Take out your list of words. Using each of them at least once, write a story describing a real or imaginary journey. The journey can take place anytime or anywhere. Be sure to use lots of details in your account.

When you're done, underline each of the words from your list. Was your word choice enriched by your use of prefixes and suffixes?

Word Choice: Adjectives and Adverbs

Adjectives and adverbs are perhaps the most popular parts of speech. Adjectives, you remember, describe a noun, while adverbs modify a verb. Although adjectives and adverbs are indispensable, they must be used with care. They should be used *only when they count.* Take a look at these sentences:

- A bird was flying in the blue sky.
- A bird was flying in the pink sky.

Now, unless there's a good reason to remind us that the sky is blue, 'blue' should be dropped. 'Pink,' however, shows us something distinctive, creating a mood.

Besides unnecessary adjectives, there are also *empty* adjectives. Which one of these sentences sounds better to you?

- The final exam was really hard.
- The final exam was unbearable.

Unbearable is far more vivid than *really hard.*

Another habit, especially among creative writers, is the overuse of adjectives. Too many adjectives will ruin a composition, just as too much salad dressing will spoil a salad. Imagine reading a story that begins like this:

-The tough men rode their dog sleds with determination through the
deep snow and freezing cold of the deserted North Pole.

Here's the same sentence with economized language:

-The men rode their dog sleds through the snow and cold of the North Pole.

Do we lose anything in this version? Wouldn't the men have to be *tough* to be sledding in the North Pole? Wouldn't they have to possess *determination?* Do we need to be reminded that the snow is *deep* or that the cold is *freezing?* These adjectives don't improve the description or add important information. Naturally, if you want to use adjectives in a sentence, *you should.* What's important is that you *decide* which ones are necessary.

Adverbs are also used too much. Often, a strong verb can eliminate the need for an adverb. Here are a few cases:

talk loudly — shout, scream, holler
run fast — sprint, dash, race
touch gently— caress
hit strongly — punch, smack
cry hard— weep, moan, blubber

Exercise

A) Each of the following sentences contains either excessive adjectives, empty adjectives or weak adverbs. Rewrite the sentences, adding precise adjectives and verbs when needed.

1. The judge spoke quietly to the prosecuting attorney.

2. The movie was great!

3. Swimming joyously, the beautiful, graceful dolphins neared our boat.

4. She's the best swimmer on the team.

5. The monkey held on tightly to the bar.

6. His car is always really dirty.

7. He is a loud-mouthed, obnoxious, offensive fellow.

8. The windy, curvy road is dangerous and scary.

9. He spoke softly; we could barely hear him.

10. That dinner tasted good.

Exercise

B) Each of the following sentences contains either excessive adjectives, empty adjectives or weak adverbs. Rewrite the sentences, adding precise adjectives and verbs when needed.

1. The thunderstorm was terrible.

2. The infant cried a lot during her vaccinations.

3. My headache really hurts.

4. The food at the new restaurant is bad.

5. She ran so fast when the wave came towards her.

6. The millionaire is very giving; he donated lots of money to the local hospital.

7. The hikers soon discovered that the trail was really hard.

8. He was so frustrated that he hit the wall over and over again.

9. White clouds floated in the blue sky as the colorful rainbow appeared.

10. She was so mad.

☞   ☞   ☞   ☞

Three Adjectives & Two Adverbs:
Practicing Precision

Here's an assignment that's challenging, fun and frustrating. Write a one page story about anything you like. Only one rule applies: *you can use only three adjectives* and *two adverbs*. When you complete the composition, read it aloud. See if everyone followed the rules!

What do you notice about your story? Did you leave much unsaid? Can the reader get a vivid feeling from the writing? Would you have preferred more adjectives and adverbs?

Note: This assignment is not intended to suggest a standard for your writing. Rather, it gives you a chance to sharpen your writing skills by paying attention to word choice.

Word Choice: Verbs

You probably know that every sentence needs at least two parts of speech: a noun and a verb. The noun is the subject of the sentence, while the verb supplies the action. Remember that the verb *gives life to the sentence.* Therefore, choosing the right verb is critical to good writing. An inaccurate or lazy verb will deaden a sentence, while a precise verb will enhance its meaning.

When speaking, we usually don't use dynamic, precise verbs. Instead, we use a limited number of common verbs. Take a look at this pair of sentences:

-The climber went up the peak.
-The climber scaled the peak.

In the first sentence, *went* is a weak verb. It doesn't capture or describe the moment. *Scaled*, on the other hand, is dynamic and appropriate to the action. Sometimes the right verb can replace an entire verb phrase:

- He wrote down the swimmers' times.
- He recorded the swimmers' times.

The phrase, *wrote down,* is not as precise as *record.* Here are three more weak verb phrases. Can you find alternatives for them?

moved around   spoke softly   had a lot of fun   laughed really hard

Exercise

A) The following paragraph contains weak verbs and verb phrases. Rewrite the sentences, exchanging weak verbs for strong ones.

The dentist came into the room when the lady shouted. Her filling had come loose and she needed a new one to be put in. But when the dentist got a drill, the lady started to shout. Then she got up fast and tried to hurry out of the room. The dentist's assistant grabbed the lady and the dentist gave her a shot to calm her down. She sat in the chair and went to sleep. Then, after using the drill, the dentist put a new filling in.

Exercise

B) This is a two-part assignment that requires a partner. First, write a long paragraph containing plenty of weak verbs. Next, rewrite one another's paragraphs, exchanging weak verbs for strong ones.

Dialect and Slang

You don't know nothing about me without you have read a book by the name of *The Adventures of Tom Sawyer;* but that ain't no matter. That book was made by Mr. Mark Twain, and he told the truth, mainly. There was things which he stretched, but mainly he told the truth. That is nothing. I never seen anybody but lied one time or another, without it was Aunt Polly, or the widow, or maybe Mary.

-Mark Twain, *Adventures of Huckleberry Finn*

The opening of *Huckleberry Finn* is a classic example of the richness of *dialect*. The narrator, Huckleberry, tells the story in *his natural speech*, Southern style. This is Huck's dialect.

We learn our dialect from the people we grow up with. Hearing their language, we adopt it as our own. There are hundreds of dialects just within the United States. Before continuing, we should distinguish between dialect and Standard English. In most countries, there is a standard dialect. In the United States, this is called Standard English, which represents "the correct way" to speak and write. However, most of us speak our own dialects, which differ in vocabulary, pronunciation and syntax.

Many of our *slang* words and expressions are born of dialect. The word 'dude,' for example, originated during the Westward movement. It meant "an Easterner or city person staying in the West." Now, in many parts, 'dude' is slang for "person," or "you."

The proper use of dialect can enrich your writing. In *Huck Finn,* the Southern dialect adds believability and charm to the character of Huck. He can say "you don't know nothing," and we understand him. This makes dialect useful for dialogue; after all, people usually don't speak in Standard English! However, in writing *avoid dialect unless it's used for a purpose.* For example, in an essay about Mercury, you don't want to say,

Mercury is the closest planet to the sun. It would be a drag to live there.

Exercise

A) Rewrite the *Huck Finn* passage, replacing Southern dialect with Standard English.

Exercise

B) In a small group, brainstorm a list of dialectical and slang phrases. Beside each word or phrase, write down its source. Where did you hear it first? Do you know its origin?

Using Dialect in a Story

Write a one-page story that uses plenty of dialect. The narrator should be close to your own age. The dialect doesn't need to be regional, *as long as it's accurate.*

Onomatopoeia and Alliteration

Onomatopoeia

bang	hiss	neigh
boom	howl	sizzle
chug	hum	thump
crackle	meow	zing
fizz	moo	zip

Each one of these words is an example of *onomatopoeia*. The sound of each suggests its meaning. Better yet, the sound *is* the meaning. Find the onomatopoeic words in these sentences:

- The restaurant is loud with the chit-chat of customers.
- Our new bird tweets a lot in the morning.
- I can hear the buzz of my dad's electric razor.

Got it? Onomatopoeia is a helpful device, but should be used *sparingly*. If you're describing a forest, beware of the temptation to fill a page with hoots, roars and caws.

Exercise

A) In a group, brainstorm a list of onomatopoeic words to add to the list above. See if you can come up with original onomatopoeic words.

Alliteration

Alliteration, the use of words that begin with the same sound, is a more sophisticated technique than onomatopoeia. Here is an example of alliteration.

- Oscar, I honor your offering with the official Award of Honesty.

Notice how many 'O' or 'AH' sounds are in the sentence. Of course, this is an extreme example. Remember, unless you're being humorous, most effective alliteration is *subtle*. By echoing sound patterns, alliteration should add rhythm and beauty to a sentence *without calling attention to itself*. Take a look at this sentence:

- The Earth is a miracle of majesty.

The alliterative phrase, *miracle of majesty*, has its own poetic quality that neither 'miracle' nor 'majesty' achieves on its own.

A Day at the Circus:
Alliteration and Onomatopoeia in Action

Using an appropriate amount of alliteration and onomatopoeia, describe a day at the circus. Be sure to include lots of details.

Clichés

Take a minute to study the list of expressions below. What do they have in common? How many have you heard before? Have you ever used any in your own writing?

accidents will happen	few and far between	on cloud nine
add insult to injury	fit as a fiddle	one in a million
better late than never	fit to be tied	quick as a wink
busy as a bee	go fly a kite	safe and sound
calm before the storm	go jump in a lake	sick as a dog
cool as a cucumber	green with envy	sink or swim
crazy as a loon	in seventh heaven	the last straw
down in the dumps	my cup of tea	under the weather

Got it? Each of these expressions is a *cliché*—an overused, unoriginal saying. Although clichés will surface in your everyday speech, they should almost always be omitted from your writing. Replace them with fresh, concise expressions.

The exception, of course, is if you're using a cliché *intentionally.* Like dialect, the proper use of clichés can enrich your writing. Because they appear in spoken English, they may have a place in dialogue. They can also be used playfully or self-consciously. Take a look at this passage:

-The '65 Chevy cruised through the summer desert. Heat mirages waved over the highway. The driver, behind the wheel all day, was under the weather.

Exercise

A) In a small group, brainstorm additions to the list of clichés above.

The Championship Game: Clichés in Action

This is a two-part assignment that will require a partner. Using plenty of clichés, write a page describing a championship contest. (Any sport will do.)

Now rewrite each other's stories, replacing the clichés with original expressions. If you want to keep any of the clichés, go ahead. However, you should be ready to justify their use.

Prepositions and Prepositional Phrases

Although you're probably familiar with the basic parts of speech—nouns, verbs, adjectives and adverbs—*prepositions* might be strangers to you. You will see, however, that they are important to good writing, allowing for sentence variety and clear description.

Prepositions are words that *show relationship between a noun or pronoun to another word in a sentence.* Look at this sentence:

- There is a lot of trash beneath the house.

The preposition, *beneath,* shows the relationship between the noun, *trash,* and the word, *house.* It tells you **where** the trash is. Here is a list of common prepositions.

about	below	inside	since
above	beneath	into	through
across	beside	like	to
after	beyond	near	toward
against	by	of	under
along	down	off	until
among	during	on	up
around	except	outside	upon
at	for	over	with
before	from	past	within

As you can see, prepositions are not limited to showing physical relationship. They can also show temporal (time-related) and logical relationships. Take a look at these examples:

- The man standing *behind* me in line was smoking a cigar. (physical)
- *Before* lunch, you should stop by and visit me. (temporal)
- *Except* for the weather, our vacation was wonderful. (logical)

Prepositional Phrases

All prepositions exist in groups of words which form *prepositional phrases.* These parts of speech begin with a preposition and end with an *object of the preposition.* Study the sentences below. The prepositional phrase is italicized; the object of the preposition is in bold print.

- The girl ran *on the* **field**.
- *Above the* **valley** soared the hawk.
- We had a lot of fun *during our* **vacation**.

Remember that the subject of the sentence is *never* in a prepositional phrase. This can be confusing, especially when a sentence has more than one prepositional phrase. Take a look at this example:

- During the concert, she sat near the manager, who was among the elite members of the audience.

Concert, manager, members and *audience* are all objects of prepositions. The subject of the sentence is *she.*

But why learn about prepositions? How are they useful? How can they help improve your writing? First of all, prepositions are essential for description. Try to describe a place without using any prepositions. Can you do it? Is the description precise? Secondly, prepositions are very useful for creating sentence variety, an important ingredient in good writing. Take a look at these examples:

- I was asleep during the train ride.
- During the train ride, I was asleep.

- The stars are shining beyond the galaxy.
- Beyond the galaxy, the stars are shining.

- We will not buy a new car until the year 2000.
- Until the year 2000, we will not buy a new car.

Notice how the sentences have a different flavor depending on where the preposition is placed. Which example do you like best? Is one more poetic than another? As you write, then, you should be aware of where you place the prepositions and how this decision affects the sentence.

Exercise

A) Drawing from the list above, write ten sentences, each containing a preposition. Next, rewrite each sentence with the preposition in a new position. *Be careful!* Sometimes moving the prepositional phrase can alter the meaning of the sentence.

- We saw the sharks in the aquarium.
- In the aquarium, we saw the sharks.

Certainly, the second sentence is faulty, unless you *want* to swim with sharks!

Describing Your House or Classroom: Prepositions in Action

Imagine you have a pen pal. He or she wants a *detailed* tour of your home. Using lots of prepositions, write a full page describing where you live. Try to create sentence variety by starting some sentences with prepositional phrases. Remember, you're trying to be as *clear* as possible! Although you will be depending on prepositions, don't overload your description. It is much better to be simple and clear than complex and confusing.

Transitions

Have you ever read an essay that's hard to follow, that leaves you wondering what you just took in? This usually happens when the writer fails to move you through the piece gently, from one idea to another. Successful essays, on the other hand, contain fluid connections between sentences and paragraphs. These connections are called *transitions*. Using them well results in smooth writing, while also securing a tone of confidence and authority. Effective transitions are a hallmark of good writing. The list below features some common transitions. Take a minute to study them.

above	consequently	in addition to	of course
after	finally	in fact	similarly
also	first, second...	last	since
although	for example	meanwhile	therefore
another	for instance	moreover	while
because	furthermore	nevertheless	yet
beside(s)	however	next	

Notice that the transitions serve different functions in ordering ideas. We can break these functions into four areas: chronological, order of importance, spatial (physical) and general (persuasive). Here is an example of each:

- Meanwhile, the cake was burning in the oven. (chronological)
- In the first place, we should thank Mrs. Smith for her donation. (importance)
- Below, you will find the treasure map. (spatial)
- Furthermore, you cannot drive until you are sixteen. (persuasive)

Much of the time, transitions exist in expressions or phrases. Here are just a few:

another reason	contrary to	more importantly
at the same time	in the first place	to begin with
as soon as	just as	rather than

Exercise

A) As you get acquainted with transitions, your writing will become more fluid and varied. It would be useful, then, to write a series of twenty sentences using different transitions and transitional phrases. Choose some of the less familiar ones!

Persuasive Writing: Transitions in Action

Transitions are especially important in persuasive writing, since they help you emphasize certain ideas. If you use *most importantly*, for example, the reader will pay special attention to what follows. Using effective transitions, write a three paragraph persuasive essay. Choose any topic you feel strongly about. Be sure to use *lots of details* to support your opinion.

Punctuation:
Colons and Semicolons

At this stage in your writing life, you're probably comfortable using periods and commas. Colons and semicolons, on the other hand, are probably unfamiliar. Have you ever used them in your writing? Do you know the difference between them? If you're a newcomer to these punctuation marks, you may find them confusing—even experienced writers find them tricky. Yet they are very helpful, adding subtlety and logic to a sentence. Before we learn their uses, keep these two things in mind:

- The only way to learn new punctuation is to *include it in your writing*. It's better to make mistakes and learn than it is to stay safe and stagnate.

- Watch for these punctuation marks in your reading. When you see a colon or semicolon, *observe* its function. This will help you gain an intuitive sense of these marks.

Colons

Colons are commonly used to introduce a list.

- We need the following items: tomatoes, carrots, juice, bread and jelly.

The colon introduces the list of foods. If it helps, think of the colon as a preview to coming attractions. Remember that colons *never* follow directly after verbs or prepositions. Here is an example of incorrect use and its remedy:

- My favorite hobbies are: stamp collecting and book reading. [incorrect]
- These are my favorite hobbies: stamp collecting and book reading. [correct]

Colons are also used to introduce long quotations *after a complete sentence.* If you're writing a research paper, this comes in handy. Here's an example:

- This statement by the president of the company proves my point: "We cannot afford to lay off workers. We must stay loyal, even if it means loss of income."

Semicolons

Beginning writers often avoid semicolons. However, they are instrumental to good writing. The semicolon is easy to understand if you look at its shape. Here's a big one:

Notice that the semicolon is made up of a period over a comma. Hence, it creates a more direct pause than a comma, but a more subtle break than a period. Here's a semicolon in action:

- It's a mystery; no one knows who ate the spaghetti.

The semicolon separates *independent* parts of the sentence. The meanings are so closely related that using a period would be too abrupt, whereas using a comma would be incorrect.

Here are some more examples of semicolons separating independent clauses. Note that you can also place transitional words after semicolons.

- He shouldn't have missed the meeting; in fact, it was the most important
  one of the year.
- That's the biggest dog I've ever seen; it must weigh 75 pounds!
- No one can stand the weather here; it's either cold or hot.
- The team played well; however, they didn't make the playoffs.

In most cases, items in a series are set off by commas. However, if the items themselves contain commas, they must be separated by semicolons.

- The meeting included the boss, Mrs. Claypool; the chairman, Dr. Smith; and the lawyer, Mr. Jones.

Exercise

A) Each of the sentences below needs either a colon or semicolon. Rewrite them, adding the appropriate punctuation mark. In some cases, the punctuation is faulty, and you'll need to restructure the sentence.

1. We'll need these tools for the project , screwdrivers, wrenches, hammers and pliers.

2. He's in a lot of trouble, he left without paying his bill.

3. My favorite dances are: the waltz, the polka, and the tango.

4. Stanley's garage is full of dynamite, it's not a safe place to visit.

5. Public speaking requires a good, strong voice, a confident, secure manner, and a classy, pleasing wardrobe.

6. The astronauts were very excited, they landed safely on Mars.

7. At the petting zoo, you must see the horse, Danger, the cat, Monster, and the bird, Chirpy.

8. She won these awards at the ceremony, most determined, most improved, and most likely to succeed.

Exercise

B) Each of the sentences below needs either a colon or semicolon. Rewrite them, adding the appropriate punctuation mark. In some cases, the punctuation is faulty, and you'll need to restructure the sentence.

1. Some people are vegetarians, some people are meat eaters.

2. After being questioned by the police, he said the following, "I'm an innocent man!"

3. George can't wait to get there, he has already packed his bags.

4. Sally works for these companies, General Electric, IBM, and AT&T.

5. The old-time theater is showing *The Godfather,* starring Marlon Brando, *Tommy,* starring Ann-Margret, and *City Lights,* starring Charlie Chaplin.

6. I'm learning a lot about astronomy, I can't wait to get a telescope.

7. The finalists in the swimming competition are: Betsy, Julie, Maria, and Nancy.

8. She wasn't listening when he asked her this question, "Will you marry me?"

Exercise

C) Using a free reading book as a reference, copy five sentences that use colons and three that use semicolons. Beside each sentence, explain why the colon or semicolon is used. Next, create six sentences of your own—three using colons, three using semicolons. Beside each one, explain why the punctuation mark is used.

Punctuation:
Parentheses and Dashes

Parentheses

Parentheses are popular among beginning writers, whether they know how to apply them or not! Often, however, they are used incorrectly. Students run into two basic problems with parentheses: when to use them and how to use punctuation with them. Let's begin with the first problem.

The function of parentheses is to add *additional but less essential* information to a sentence or a paragraph. Don't use parentheses if the words in parentheses are important to the meaning of the sentence. If you're not sure, try removing the parentheses and seeing if the meaning remains the same. In this example, parentheses are used wrongly:

   - The best skier (who went on the trip) is Gus.

Who went on the trip is essential because it modifies the statement *The best skier.* Otherwise, Gus would be the best skier, period! Now let's look at some correct sentences:

   - We watched "Little Women" (the earlier version) last night.
   - I woke up at 5:30, but then I realized I could sleep in (it was Sunday).

Notice that each sentence would be complete *without* the words in the parentheses; although the information is relevant, it's not necessary.

Parentheses & punctuation

Study the examples above. Notice that parentheses *do not require any additional punctuation* around them. Writers often make the mistake of adding commas before and after parentheses. However, if the words enclosed in parentheses need a punctuation mark, it should be applied. Here are a few examples.

   - The cartoonist (her name is Debbie, I believe) is starting a new project.
   - The sheriff finally arrived (we waited forty minutes!).
   - My mom serves vegetables (do we always have to eat them?) every night.

Note how a complete sentence can be included within the parentheses. Also notice that the appropriate punctuation marks are placed *within* the parentheses. The sentence, meanwhile, carries on with its own natural punctuation.

Dashes

Dashes are similar to parentheses in that they indicate a pause or shift in a sentence. However, unlike parentheses, dashes *emphasize* what follows. Take a look at this sentence:

- "Yes," said the nurse, "you're pregnant—with twins!"

In this example, a surprise statement is introduced by a single dash. Here's another example:

- He came home drunk—it wasn't the first time—at midnight.

This sentence includes dashes instead of parentheses because *the information is relevant and dramatic.*

Note: There should be no spaces between the dash and the word preceding or following it. Also, unless you're working with a word processor that has a dash, the dash should be typed as two hyphens, like this: ——.

Exercise

A) Combine each pair of sentences by using either parentheses or dashes. You may need to eliminate words.

1. Our annual vacation to Lake Tahoe was terrific. It was the fourth year in a row.

2. The playoff game was canceled. What a drag.

3. She noticed he wasn't breathing. Thank God she was a doctor.

4. Chewing tobacco is popular in these parts. About 35% of the people do it.

5. The quote you're looking for is fascinating. It's on page 73.

6. The movie went way over budget. We spent an extra 17 million dollars.

7. Lisa is coming to the family party. She's my little sister.

8. I was surprised at his manner after the accident. He was cheerful, lighthearted, and talkative.

Exercise

B) Combine each pair of sentences by using either parentheses or dashes. You may need to eliminate words.

1. The countdown to liftoff stopped abruptly. How disappointing.

2. My dear friend is coming to visit. She's from Texas.

3. Discuss the passage carefully. It's on page 198.

4. This is your last warning. Next time you'll be grounded.

5. Brian ate too much licorice during the movie. He ate about 13 pieces, I think.

6. Dragons don't exist, but some people feel they once did. I'm talking about dragons like the ones in Chinese mythology.

7. The Declaration of Independence went through many changes before it was signed. It was signed in 1776.

8. I'm sorry. I didn't know you were fired.

☞   ☞   ☞   ☞

Exercise

C) Using a free reading book as a reference, copy five sentences that use parentheses and three that use a dash(es). Beside each sentence, explain why parentheses or dashes are used.

Now create ten sentences of your own, five using parentheses and five using dashes. Beside each one, explain why the punctuation mark is used.

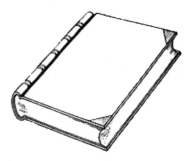

Fragments & Run-ons

Fragments and run-ons are among the most conspicuous and unfortunate of all writing mistakes. A *fragment* is simply an incomplete sentence. A *run-on* is when two or more sentences appear as one:

- The man who stood in the doorway. [fragment]
- She opened the folder, there was a note inside it. [run-on]

Interestingly, if the word *who* was omitted from the first sentence, the sentence would be complete. Why? To answer this, we need to understand the difference between dependent and independent clauses. An *independent clause* can stand alone as a complete thought and a complete sentence. It contains a subject and a verb. Here are two independent clauses:

- He was nearly eighty years old.
- He was in great shape.

Of course, independent clauses can be combined:

- He was nearly eighty years old, but he was in great shape.

A run-on sentence happens when two independent clauses are combined incorrectly. Here are two examples:

- I went to school, I've been busy all day.
- The weather has been great, it's been sunny all week.

The sentences can be repaired easily by combining the independent clauses:

- I went to school, so I've been busy all day.
- The weather has been great; it's been sunny all week.

As you can see, run-ons are easy to fix. If you're having a hard time bringing independent clauses together, make them into two sentences separated by a period. Now let's take a look at fragments.

Fragments are incomplete sentences. Often they are made up of *dependent clauses*. Although dependent clauses have a subject and a verb, they do not form a complete thought. Here are a few cases:

- Because she won't go fishing.
- When the newspaper gets delivered.

Notice that the first word of each clause makes it dependent—each sentence needs more information to be a complete thought. However, strike the first words and you have two complete sentences! By following the thought through, we make whole sentences:

- Because she won't go fishing, her boyfriend is staying home.
- When the newspaper gets delivered, I'll know who won the election.

Exercise

A) The following paragraph contains plenty of fragments and run-ons. Rewrite the passage, making the necessary corrections.

> He looked at his face in the mirror, he didn't like what he saw. Two giant hairs were growing on top of his nose. Which were disgusting. Especially the top one, it was crooked and eerie. He needed to do something, he had a date that night. Unless she had canceled. Which he knew was quite possible, if he hadn't noticed these hairs earlier. So, he plucked out both hairs, it really hurt! But it was worth it, they fell in love.

A Mystery Object:
Fragments & Run-ons in Action

As you know, a good way to learn to recognize mistakes is to practice them. Using fragments and run-ons with regularity, write a one page story about what happens when you find a mystery object. You can find the object anywhere; just remember that when you first find it, *you don't know its powers!*

When you're done, exchange your story with a partner's. Rewrite each other's accounts, correcting the fragments and run-ons.

Parallel Construction

/ /

In mathematics, parallel lines (like the ones above) must maintain the same relationship, or distance, to each other. In architecture, a house relying on evenly-spaced columns must have *parallel construction*. Interestingly, in writing, *parallel construction* has the same quality of relationship. It means that each item in a list or a series of expressions should have a matching form. Here is an example of parallel construction:

- The king raised a family, led an army, and ruled a nation.

Notice that each of the three phrases has similar construction: a verb, article and noun. Although the items don't need to be identical, their general forms must be alike. Here's the same sentence without parallel construction:

- The king raised a family, led an army, and he was very popular.

By reintroducing the subject, the third phrase breaks the established form. This is called *faulty parallelism*. Although the sentence still makes sense, it is grammatically unsound.

But what is parallelism used for? How can it help refine your writing? First of all, parallelism is an excellent tool for sentence combining. Look at the following sentences. Notice how the first group can be combined by using parallel construction:

- When we visit the city, I want to go shopping. I want to eat sushi. I also want to walk in the park.
- When we visit the city, I want to go shopping, eat sushi, and walk in the park.

Parallelism is linked to repetition; used effectively, it can be both forceful and poetic. Take a look at the opening paragraph of J.R.R. Tolkien's classic, *The Hobbit*.

In a hole in the ground there lived a hobbit. Not a nasty, dirty wet hole, filled with the ends of worms and an oozy smell, nor yet a dry, bare, sandy hole with nothing in it to sit down on or to eat: it was a hobbit-hole, and that means comfort.

The second sentence is a lively example of parallel construction. The repetition of form establishes rhythm and humor while setting us up for the final, strong statement: *it was a hobbit-hole.*

Before we begin our exercises, let's look at one more example of faulty parallelism. What's wrong with this sentence?

- I had a nightmare about goblins, ballerinas, and the giant ants attacked.

Got it? The first two items are parallel nouns. The third item changes the series by introducing the verb, *attacked.* Now let's fix the nightmare.

- I had a nightmare about goblins, ballerinas and giant ants.

Exercise

A) Each of the sentences below contains faulty parallelism. Rewrite them, establishing parallel construction.

1. We need these office supplies: paper, staples, folders, and we need more envelopes.

2. Depending on the distance of the trip, the amount of passengers, and if they departed on time, my relatives should arrive around noon.

3. Jerusalem is an ancient city that has housed Hebrews, Romans, Ottomans, and the British were there.

4. I've looked everywhere—below the refrigerator, the cupboard, and above the oven.

5. Our school received funding because the math scores are improving, the speech team is winning and everyone likes the principal.

6. The desert was beautiful: the wildflowers were blooming, the sky was clear, and I had a fun time on the drive.

7. When I was young, I tried on several images: I was a long-haired hippie, a clean-cut athlete, and I liked to study a lot.

8. This beach—with its warmth, quiet, and lots of space—is my favorite place.

Exercises

B) Each of the sentences below contains faulty parallelism. Rewrite them, establishing parallel construction.

1. Nobody knows my name, my age, or how tall I am.

2. The lizard has black stripes, a short tail, and its tongue is long.

3. Too much leisure breeds laziness, a boring life, and lethargy.

4. She is admired, everyone likes her, and she is bright.

5. The rainstorms come in the winter, spring, and there are summer ones, too.

6. We need the following equipment for our backpacking trip: an ice pick, a first-aid kit, and we have to carry three tents.

7. The kids hid under the sofa, under the bed, and crouching behind the door.

8. The house has tall windows, a long driveway and its gates are antique.

☞   ☞   ☞   ☞

What I Would Do With $1,000,000:
Parallel Construction in Action

Imagine that you wake up tomorrow morning to find that you've won one million dollars in a sweepstakes! The only catch is that you *have to* spend it all in one week, and your spending spree must include at least one vacation. Using lots of parallel construction, write at least one page explaining how you would exhaust your riches.

When you're done, exchange your piece with a classmate's. Proofread each other's work, making sure the parallel constructions are accurate.

Extension

Using a free reading book as a reference, copy down three passages that use parallel construction.

Below each passage, explain why the author used parallel construction. How does it affect the content? In your opinion, are the parallels effective?

Misplaced & Dangling Modifiers

To modify means "to change," or "to alter." In composition, *modifiers* are often used to add information and to create sentence variety.

- The dolls in the display are for sale.

In this example, the prepositional phrase *in the display* tells us more about the dolls. The phrase can be removed from the sentence without making the sentence incomplete. Here's another example:

- My cousin, who is ten years old, is coming to visit.

Who is ten years old modifies *cousin,* but it is not needed to form a complete sentence. Of course, you don't want too many modifiers. Take a look at this account:

Today, after the sound of the two o'clock bell, the mayor, who had to come all the way from across town, where he had a meeting, will speak about the new taxes, a topic which will, no doubt, create a great deal of fuss among the citizens.

Although this sentence is grammatically correct, it is stringy and ineffective. The abundance of modifiers weakens the description. It would sound much better as two or three sentences.

Misplaced Modifiers

One common and entertaining writing error is the *misplaced modifier.* Here's an example:

- At the age of seven, my uncle taught me how to ride my bike.

What's wrong with this sentence? Got it? This would have to be a pretty young uncle! This is a simple solution:

- When I was seven, my uncle taught me how to ride my bike.

Here's another example:

- We saw an eagle soaring above the peaks looking through our binoculars.

Either the eagle stole their binoculars, or the sentence has a misplaced modifier! You can correct the sentence by repositioning the modifier:

- Looking though our binoculars, we saw an eagle soaring above the peaks.

Remember that *modifiers should be as near as possible to the word they modify.* Otherwise, the sentence will be unclear and, quite possibly, rather strange!

Sometimes, modifiers have nothing to describe. These are called *dangling modifiers*. Here is one example:

- Having played soccer all day, the field looked worn down.

Certainly, the field didn't play soccer all day. But who did? The sentence doesn't tell us. Here's one solution:

- The field looked worn down after the team played soccer all day.

Exercise

A) Each of the following sentences contains either a misplaced or dangling modifier. Rewrite the sentences correctly.

1. We saw the ice cream truck bicycling home from school.

2. Broken and old, he sold the car to the dump.

3. After brushing her teeth for the first time, my mom gave my baby sister a kiss.

4. Having landed on the moon, the world was changed.

5. His business partner is a man who owns properties named Ralph.

6. While swinging the bat, the fans cheered.

7. Julian watched the meteor showers camping on the mountain.

8. Leaving for Tennessee, her luggage was left in the taxi.

Exercise

B) Each of the following sentences contains either a misplaced or dangling modifier. Rewrite the sentences correctly.

1. Between the night stand and the dresser, we should think about putting a bookcase.

2. To join the rehearsals, permission slips must be signed.

3. While running on the beach, the cartwheel made him twist his ankle.

4. Having worked all day, a rest was needed.

5. We saw a frog rowing our canoe across the lake.

6. After getting ready for the play, the curtain wouldn't open.

7. Upset by the bad weather, the tennis tournament was canceled.

8. Dreaming of a werewolf, the yapping of coyotes woke me.

☞   ☞   ☞   ☞

Writing a Soap Opera:
Misplaced & Dangling Modifiers in Action

Using plenty of misplaced and dangling modifiers, write a one page soap opera full of plot twists and romance. The result will provide lots of laughs!

After reading your story aloud, exchange it with a classmate's. Correct all the misplaced and dangling modifiers.

Repetition vs. Repetitious

Repetition is a double-edged sword. Used properly, it will add rhythm, logic and authority to your writing. Used inappropriately, it will make your writing boring and ineffectual; in other words, it will become *repetitious.* But what makes for skilled repetition? How can you avoid becoming repetitious?

Have you ever seen a courtroom drama on TV or in the movies? Remember when the lawyer delivers a powerful closing speech? Usually, the speech has a great deal of repetition. It might sound something like this:

> The defendant is a good man. Has he ever been convicted of a crime? Has he ever abandoned his family or failed to care for his loved ones? Has he ever done anything but good for his community? The answer, ladies and gentlemen of the jury, is no, no, no!

Here, repetition works by *reinforcing* the lawyer's point. Each of the lawyer's statements is distinct and justified, creating a tone of authority.

Now let's shift to the dangers of repetition. First of all, there's the repetition of ideas. Ideas should be restated only for emphasis. Otherwise, you should make your point and then move on. If you're reporting on the hazards of smoking, for example, don't discuss second-hand smoke in every section of your essay.

Repetitious writing also creeps into sentences. Take a look at this example:

> - I'm so tired and sleepy. Gosh, I'm exhausted. I can barely keep my eyes open. I'm ready to go to bed.

Not only is this writing repetitious, it's also irritating! The above sentences should simply state,

> - I'm sleepy and ready for bed.

So, when revising your work, beware of repetitious writing. Always ask yourself if your statements are necessary and if they are saying something new.

Exercise

A) This is a two-part exercise. First, write a long paragraph marred by repetitious writing. Next, write a paragraph that uses effective repetition.

Sentence Combining

A Word about Revision

Any dedicated writer would tell you that *revision* is critical to successful composition. In fact, many writers spend more time revising than writing. But what is revision? Why is it important?

Revision is simply *rewriting*. (*Revision* means "to look again.") When you revise, you read with a critical eye, attentive to all areas of writing: mechanics, spelling, grammar, style, structure, meaning, tone, and so forth. Beginning writers often resist revision, especially if they're relying on "inspiration" to carry them through. But unless you're a genius, skilled writing requires revision.

The more devoted you are to revision, the more effective your writing. Once you see the results firsthand, you'll begin to appreciate and even enjoy the process. Let's start with sentence combining, an extremely useful writing skill.

Sentence Combining

Most first drafts suffer from overwriting. This is natural, since the writer is busy formulating thoughts and setting them down. Although overwriting involves wordiness, it also means using too many sentences. The remedy for this is sentence combining. Take a look at the following sentences:

- The squirrel is eating an acorn. The acorn is small. We are watching the squirrel.

The writer is using too many sentences to get an idea across. You've probably already combined these sentences in your head. Here's one option:

- We are watching the squirrel eat the small acorn.

Notice how sentence combining results in fluid, concise writing. Look at these sentences:

- We watched the movie. We went home. Then we had a snack and went to bed.
- After watching the movie, we went home, had a snack and went to bed.

In this case, adding the preposition *after* was helpful. Of course, there are often a variety of ways sentences can be combined. Take this example:

- A map is the traveler's best friend. It is essential on road trips.
- A map, the traveler's best friend, is essential on road trips.

Got it? Let's look at one more combining option:

- Mrs. Bernstein wanted a steak. She was very hungry.
- Mrs. Bernstein, who wanted a steak, was very hungry.

Here, the pronoun *who* allowed the sentences to merge smoothly. Other helpful pronouns include *whom, whose, that* and *which*.

Finally, remember that you don't *always* want to combine sentences. Sometimes a sentence needs to stand alone.

- He was a strong man. He had a good heart.

The sentences emphasize the man's good heart.

Exercise

A) Combine each group into one or two sentences. Use a variety of combining strategies.

1. Mrs. Reyes wrote a play. The play was about her family. The play was excellent.

2. A sailor should always be aware of weather conditions. This ensures a safe trip.

3. No one would talk to him. He was always bitter.

4. Janet is eighteen. She attends Harvard College. She wants to major in psychology.

5. The volcano is about to erupt. The volcano is ancient.

6. Bradly is tall and thin. He likes to read. He likes to play guitar.

7. We went to the diner. Then we went to the lake. We like to swim there at night.

8. He shouted at his dog. His dog wouldn't come. His dog was stubborn.

Exercise

B) Combine each group into one or two sentences. Use a variety of combining strategies.

1. The salad is fresh from the garden. It has avocado mixed in. The avocado is ripe.

2. Houdini was a great magician. He could escape from chains.

3. There is grass on the mountain top. The herd of elk lives there.

4. After playing tennis, we went to school. At school we met Jonathan.

5. Sherman is sweet. He is our neighbor's cat. He doesn't have a tail.

6. She wrote to the president. Her letter was ignored.

7. You will need Indian spices for that recipe. You will also need butter and salt.

8. The bookstore was closed. Today is a holiday.

The First Thirty Minutes of My Day: Sentence Combining in Action

This is a two-part exercise. First, freewrite a page about the first half-hour of your day. Describe brushing your teeth, eating breakfast, bathing, and so forth. Don't stop to edit or revise. Afterwards, rewrite the piece, combining as many sentences as possible.

Can a Story Be One Sentence? More Sentence Combining in Action

Gabriel Garcia Marquez, winner of the Nobel prize for literature, is the author of a short story called *The Last Voyage of the Ghost Ship*. Like most of his stories, *Ghost Ship* is rich with imagery, passion and magic. Its unique feature, however, is that it is five pages long and contains *one* sentence.

Now it's your turn to give it a try. In *one* sentence, write a one page story. Before beginning, review the use of *semicolons, parentheses* and *dashes*. Good luck! Be sure to read your story to a friend.

Note: If you find the assignment highly frustrating, feel free to write the story in two or three sentences.

Sentence Variety

In becoming a skilled writer, the importance of sentence variety cannot be underestimated. By learning to change the rhythm, length, and structure of your sentences, you gain mastery over your writing, creating depth and nuance. Let's take a look at two strategies for creating sentence variety.

Sentence Patterns

Here's an experiment: Find one of your essays or stories and calculate the percentage of sentences beginning with a subject followed by a verb. Don't be surprised if your answer is in the 70%-90% range. This is because the most common sentence pattern is the subject-verb pattern. Here's an example:

- The rhino charged the car.

Rhino is the subject, and *charged* is the verb. Unfortunately, many writers never go beyond this subject-verb pattern. Thus, their writing becomes predictable and flat. Let's explore some sentence pattern alternatives by rewriting the opening of the above sentence. Read each of the examples out loud.

- Enraged, the rhino charged the car. [Adjective.]
- Despite its docile personality, the rhino charged the car. [Prepositional phrase.]
- Because the man shouted, the rhino charged the car. [Dependent clause.]

Notice that each sentence pattern produces a different *rhythm*. Also, note how the subject and verb still remain adjacent to each other in these examples. Now let's look at a couple of examples when the subject and verb are separated.

- The rhino, enraged, charged the car.
- The rhino, despite its docile personality, charged the car.

As you can see, there are lots of possibilities for sentence patterns. We have seen only a few. Be sure to pay attention to sentence patterns when you revise your work.

Sentence Length

Sentence variety also includes *sentence length*. Too many short sentences or too many long sentences make for dull reading. Long sentences are usually preferable for lists or descriptions, and a variety of sentence patterns will add rhythm to long sentences. Short sentences are normally more emphatic. After establishing a rhythm with longer sentences, a short statement adds drama and force. Study the following paragraph. Notice the variety of sentence patterns and sentence length.

Undisciplined and mischievous, the puppy was trouble from day one. Ruben decided a trip to the wilderness would help sober the pup. But the moment they began hiking, the puppy broke free. Desperately, Ruben chased it through the woods. Although he ran at top speed, Ruben didn't have a chance to catch the dog. Finally, despite all his efforts to train the dog, despite all his hopes for a loyal friend, Ruben surrendered. He drove home.

The final statement, *He drove home,* is forceful because it follows a series of longer sentences. These sentences contain a variety of sentence patterns. However, if the entire paragraph followed a subject-verb pattern, *He drove home* would not carry the same drama.

Exercise

A) Adding adjectives, prepositions, and dependent clauses, create sentence variety for each of the subject-verb sentences below.

1. The clown juggled six lemons.

2. A crowd gathered around the exhibit.

3. Susan bought a new car.

4. Todd and Ellen are having twins.

5. The dentist jumped for joy.

6. The apples fell from the tree.

7. Jeremy applied for the job.

8. The movie was four hours long!

9. I sailed the boat.

10. The alarm sounded all day long.

Exercise

B) Using a free reading book for reference, copy a paragraph that exhibits sentence variety. Below the passage, explain how the author makes use of sentence patterns and sentence length.

Revising a Recent Essay or Story: Sentence Variety in Action

Rewrite at least one page of an essay or story that you've written. Paying attention to sentence length and patterns, create an appropriate amount of sentence variety.

Stream-of-Consciousness: Medicine for Writers

Although good writing requires careful thought and hard work, being *overly* concerned with finding the perfect word or sentence structure can be detrimental. You don't want to lose touch with the fun and discovery of writing! One way to break the cycle of "all work and no play" is by writing a stream-of-consciousness piece.

The instructions here are simple: begin writing and ***don't stop!*** Disregard all rules of grammar, syntax, punctuation and so forth. The idea is to allow expression, to gather momentum and see what surfaces. If you run out of things to say, *keep on writing.* If you're stuck, you can write "I'm stuck" over and over again! Sooner or later, you'll break out of it and discover a rhythm.

Besides taking a break from the "laws" of composition, stream-of-consciousness writing can help you discover and vent your feelings. You might be surprised to find yourself getting emotional as you write, or writing about a person or event you haven't thought of in years.

Twenty minutes of writing is recommended for beginners, although you should feel free to go on longer.

Simile and Metaphor

Writing is description. Whether you're clarifying an opinion or creating a setting, your ultimate goal is to *describe.* We've already learned how precise word choice will enhance your writing. Now we can look at *similes* and *metaphors,* two useful devices for description.

Similes and metaphors are figures of speech that make comparisons. They are called *figures of speech* because they are imaginative rather than literal. Similes, for example, make comparisons by using either *like, as,* or *than.*

- Her smile is like a rainbow.
- He is as fast as a cheetah.
- The group laughed more than hyenas at a party!

Got it? Although smiles are not literally like rainbows, both share a quality of joy; no one runs the speed of a cheetah, but the comparison stirs our imagination; hyenas don't have parties (at least, not that we know of!) but the comparison adds humor.

Metaphors also make comparisons, but they do not use *like, as,* or *than.* Instead, they assert that one thing *is* another thing. Again, this leap is imaginary. Here are a couple of metaphors:

- The tears of God rained down on the funeral.
- School is the waiting room of life.

Notice how the metaphors convey a mood. Raindrops are *not* the tears of God, but if you're having a terrible day, they might as well be. If school is intolerable, it feels like a waiting room!

Some writers employ *extended metaphors.* An extended metaphor develops beyond a single sentence. Read this passage from John Knowles', *A Separate Peace.*

> So the war swept over like a wave at the seashore, gathering power and size as it bore on us, overwhelming in its rush, seemingly inescapable, and then at the last moment eluded by a word from Phineas; I had simply ducked, that was all, and the wave's concentrated power had hurtled harmlessly overhead, no doubt throwing others roughly up on the beach, but leaving me peaceably treading water as before. I did not stop to think that one wave is inevitably followed by another even larger and more powerful, when the tide is coming in.

Notice how the simile, *like a wave,* is transformed into an extended metaphor. The wave's meaning expands until it finally foreshadows upcoming events. Like all figures of speech, metaphors and extended metaphors are best used sparingly.

Exercise: Similes

A) Here's a fun way to invent original similes. In groups of three or four, gather some everyday objects, such as pencils, backpacks, and lunch bags. Now brainstorm similes for each object, giving the *reasoning* behind each simile: *A pencil is like a needle—it can hurt as well as heal.*

Exercise: Metaphors

B) In the same group, one person volunteers a noun. Each member writes down a metaphor using the word. If someone says, *building,* you might write, *The building is a labyrinth.* Afterwards, compare your metaphors. Be ready to explain your comparison. Remember, the comparison needs to be rational; it should enhance meaning, not detract from it.

Exercise

C) Using a free reading book as a reference, copy at least one simile and one metaphor. (You might want to use a book of poetry.) Beside each figure of speech, explain its meaning and evaluate its effectiveness. Did it enhance meaning? Is it poetic?

Planet Zorbon:
Metaphors and Similes in action

You and a friend just landed on Planet Zorbon, 12,000 light years from Earth. First, *without* using similes or metaphors, write a long paragraph describing Zorbon.

Now exchange your description with a classmate's. Embellish each other's writing with lots of similes and metaphors.

Tone

Let's see if we discover what *tone is* by doing a theater game. The rules of the game are simple. Find a partner and decide on a scene to improvise. (You might want to take suggestions from classmates.) During the scene, *you're only allowed to say your partner's first name.* Your job is to capture the mood and action of the scene. For example, if Mark is surprised to see Julia, he would say "Julia!" If Julia isn't sure she recognizes him, she would answer, "Mark?"

You'll probably be surprised how much meaning you can convey relying on only two words. How did you do it? The answer is *tone.* By changing the tone of your voice, the meaning of the scene shifted. In writing, the tone is equally significant—it reflects the writer's attitude towards the content. Therefore, it's important to be *aware* of the tone you've established.

Exercise

A) Let's practice recognizing tone. One way to discover it is to imagine the author reading out loud. How would her voice sound? Kind? Mad? Thoughtful? Write down the tone of each sentence below.

- Give me a break! How do you expect me to finish this project in one day?

- Open the manual to page 14. Refer to rule number 176.B for details on assembly.

- Duncan's hair is a tumbleweed, Mom's yelling at the dog, and the mailman, God bless him, is drunk again.

Exercise

B) The tone of an accomplished writer is not always easy to define; it might take several words to describe. That's because you're hearing the writer's *voice*, unique and rich with meaning. Read this passage from Ursula K. LeGuin's, *A Wizard of Earthsea.* Write at least three words that describe the tone.

> All that day, all that night they went driven by the powerful wind of magery over the great swells of ocean, eastward. Ged kept watch from dusk till dawn, for in darkness the force that drew or drove him grew stronger yet. Always he watched ahead, though his eyes in the moonless night could see no more than the painted eyes aside the boat's blind prow. By daybreak his dark face was grey with weariness, and he was so cramped with cold that he could hardly stretch out to rest. He said whispering, "hold the magewind from the west, Estarriol," and then he slept.

Two Voices on the First Day of School: Tone in Action

Write a long paragraph about a student's first day of school. Be sure to establish a strong tone. The student might be nervous, happy, excited, petrified, angry, and so on.

When you're done, exchange your piece with a classmate's. Now, rewrite the paragraph by *changing the tone.* Make the student have a different attitude about school.

Extension

This exercise requires a partner. Together, find three books you admire. Read a passage from each book.

Now each of you defines the tone separately. Afterwards, compare your notes.

Style

So far, we've studied some of the elements of good writing: choosing concise words, varying sentence structure, using parallel construction, and so forth. Just as a musician must learn scales, a writer must master the basics. Only afterwards is the artist free to develop his own distinct *style.* Now that you've touched on the basics, it's your turn to experiment with style.

There are many features that contribute to writing style. Use one of your favorite authors to try to discover these features. Referring to a book you love, answer the following questions about style:

- Are there lots of adjectives? Are the verbs strong?
- Are the sentences long or short? Does their structure vary? What structure does the writer prefer?
- Are the paragraphs long or short? Does their structure vary?
- What sort of *rhythm* is achieved within the sentences and paragraphs?
- What's the *flavor* or *tone* of the writing? Is it intellectual, poetic, authoritative, humorous?
- What kind of language does the author use? Formal? Informal? Does the writer use dialect or slang?
- Are the descriptions highly detailed or more general?
- Is the emphasis on plot? character? setting?
- Is there lots of dialogue?
- Does the writer use lots of devices, like imagery? Metaphor? Symbolism?

Of course, it's not easy to define the style of an accomplished writer. A great writer creates a style and language particular only to her work. This style is *earned* through lots of effort and self-honesty.

Exercise

A) Let's see if you can define your own writing style. Referring to a story that you've recently written, answer the questions listed above. Feel free to add to the list of questions.

Imitating a Writer:
Style in Action

This is an entertaining and helpful exercise that will acquaint you with the nuances of style. Simply write a page imitating your favorite author. You can choose from poetry, fiction, or nonfiction. Before beginning, identify the qualities of the writing style. Feel free to exaggerate these features. Afterwards, read your piece to the class. The results are often humorous!

Paragraphs:
The Building Blocks of Composition

Now that you've worked on composing sentences and choosing words, it's time to take the next crucial step: creating paragraphs. A *paragraph* is a group of sentences relating to a main idea. Unless your sentences are grouped into coherent paragraphs, they lose their effectiveness.

But what makes for good paragraphs? When should you create them? Do they all need to be the same length?

You might be familiar with the model for nonfiction paragraphs. The *topic sentence* should introduce the main idea while grabbing the reader. This is followed by *supporting sentences* which develop the main idea by providing details. Finally, a *concluding sentence* restates the main idea in an interesting way. Let's take a look at a well-structured paragraph.

> Our small town, once humble and friendly, has lost its charm. Only a few years ago, I could stroll down Main Street without hearing the sound of traffic. I used to buy all my products from the General Store. Now I have to drive five miles to the Superstore. Worst of all, I have to lock my house in the evening, for fear of criminals. Maybe I'll move elsewhere, to a small town that hasn't been spoiled.

The *topic sentence* does its job by introducing the main idea. The details support the writer's feeling that his town has "lost its charm." The concluding sentence reinforces the opening thought.

Of course, paragraphs are not isolated units; the disgruntled man in this story could begin packing and then catch a bus to the nearest small town. In that case, the writer must continue to create paragraphs.

Always remember that paragraphs, like sentences, should have variety. Some paragraphs, for example, might be only one sentence long. Like short sentences, these provide punch and emphasis. However, it's important to remember that *each paragraph must have its own coherence*. Beware of overlapping main ideas in one paragraph.

Exercise

A) Find a published essay that you admire. First, explain the paragraph breaks. Try to identify a pattern in the length and emphasis of the paragraphs.

Next, isolate a long paragraph. Can you locate the topic sentence? Is there sentence variety? Would you have written the paragraph differently?

☞   ☞   ☞   ☞

Portrait of a Hero:
Paragraphing in Action

This is a two-part assignment. First, write a page-long essay about one of your heroes. Create *at least* three coherent paragraphs. You might want to address the following questions:

• What is this person famous for?

• In your opinion, why is this person heroic?

• What qualities does this person have that you admire?

• What qualities do you share with this person?

On a separate sheet of paper, explain your choice of paragraph breaks.

Copying

Today's assignment might seem a little strange. In fact, you'll probably resist it. However, if you follow it through, your writing stands to improve greatly.

Painters often learn style and medium by copying famous works, just as musicians play great songs in order to sharpen their own skills. In short, it makes sense to copy good art. Writing is no exception.

The assignment here is simple: Copy, *by hand,* one page from a published essay. Don't do anything else while you're writing—don't listen to music or watch TV or talk on the telephone. Keep focused on the process.

You're probably wondering how this exercise is beneficial. To begin with, copying introduces you *firsthand* to the style of a good writer. Style, punctuation, and vocabulary you aren't accustomed to flows from your pen. Hopefully, the writer's skill rubs off.

Of course, this exercise won't suddenly transform you into a great writer! But it does provide a very direct way of learning. In fact, copying work is a useful exercise at *any* time. Although you might find yourself imitating the writer for a while, if you keep working, you'll discover your own voice.

When you complete your copying, write about the author's style. What are the elements that you admire? Which ones could you do without?

Writing a Boring Piece

Begin this experiment by finding an excerpt from a poem, essay or novel that you find boring. In a few words, explain why it's boring. Is the tone uninteresting? Is the plot dull? Does it lack clarity? Is the language too sentimental, abstract, or conversational?

By identifying what makes the piece boring to you, you can avoid these pitfalls in your own writing. This leads to our assignment, which is bound to produce laughs and controversy.

Try to write a boring piece. It's a lot harder than you think! Here are some rules:

- It has to be a poem, essay or story. No instruction manuals or encyclopedia entries.

- It has to make sense. You can't be deliberately nonsensical or write the same sentence over and over again.

- It should be well-written; although this is an experiment, you should practice good writing.

- It has to be at least one page.

When everyone is done, each student takes turns reading his piece to the class. On a scale of 1-10, the class rates the composition's "degree of boredom."

Hopefully, this assignment will refine your writing sensibility. Always remember this: *how you write is as important as **what** you write.* Just because your content is dull, it doesn't mean your tone will be. Likewise, even fascinating material can be made dull by bad writing.

Brainstorming and Outlining

Suppose you want to build your dream house. You've picked a lovely plot of land and you're ready to begin. What's the first step? Do you build right away? Hopefully not, unless you've already designed the house. Are the rooms measured? Do you know where the kitchen will go and its dimensions? Without the right planning, your dream house will look like a nightmare, with uneven walls and triangular rooms.

This same principle of planning applies to writing. We call it *outlining.* Put simply, outlining is the process of *ordering ideas.* Unfortunately, beginning writers often resist outlining , and end up with uneven, disorganized compositions. But what are the benefits of outlining? How is it done?

First of all, outlining will *save time.* Once you have all your ideas ordered, you can get on with the task of writing. Otherwise, you'd have to write and order your ideas simultaneously—what a strain! Do the groundwork first, then get on with the building.

But most importantly, a thorough outline ensures a logical, interesting composition. Each idea is related, adding depth to the main topic or thesis [see next page]. A disorganized paper, on the other hand, weakens the power of the ideas it presents. Now let's take a look at the steps for creating an outline.

Brainstorming

Before beginning your outline, you want to generate supporting ideas. This is done by *brainstorming*, or jotting down *everything* that comes to your mind about your topic. This includes facts, opinions, theories, and so forth. There are lots of ways to do this. You can simply make a list on lined paper, or you can write all over a piece of large paper, connecting related thoughts. Its always beneficial to brainstorm in groups. Whatever your approach, the key is to *flood yourself with ideas.*

Exercise

A) In a small group, spend twenty to thirty minutes brainstorming ideas for one of the topics listed below. Remember, jot down *everything* that comes to mind, even if it seems irrelevant or silly. (Feel free to choose your own topic.) *Be sure to save your paper.* You'll need it later.

- kids in the workplace

- violence on television

- immigration policy

- the need for recycling

The Formal Outline

After brainstorming your topic, you're ready to begin an outline. Here is a model of a formal outline. Take a minute to study it.

Thesis Statement (includes introduction)

I. Main Topic
  A. Subtopic
      1. Supporting point
        (a. detail)
        (b. detail)
      2. Supporting point
      3. Supporting point

  B. Subtopic
      1. Supporting point
      2. Supporting point

II. Main Topic
        (Same as above)

Conclusion

Notice that the outline begins with a *thesis* which states your main idea; it tells the reader what your composition is about. This statement is included in the introduction, which, like the topic sentence of a paragraph, should interest the reader. Next, the Roman numeral I signifies the first *main topic*. Depending on the length and depth of your paper, you might have two, three, or even four main topics. While the main topics support the thesis, they must also be broad enough to merit their own lists of supporting details. This is where the *subtopics* enter. Subtopics, indicated by capital letters, group the main topic into separate categories. Each of these is followed by *supporting points*, or details. (If these details require further support, add lower case letters.) Again, the amount of details will vary.

Continuing to the next main topic, simply repeat the process. When you're done, be sure to add a *conclusion*. This will remind you to summarize your thesis at the end of your paper. Here's a sample section of an outline. Notice how the ideas reinforce one another. Also, note the movement from *general to specific*.

Thesis Statement: The world is endangered by overpopulation

I. Main Topic...........depletion of resources
  A. Subtopic...........running out of energy sources
      1. Supporting point..........oil reserves are running out
        a. Detail..........statistics on oil reserves in the U.S.A.
        b. Detail..........statistics on oil reserves in the Middle East
        c. Detail..........statistics on oil reserves in U.S.A. and Middle East ten
          years ago

At first glance, the formal outline might appear intimidating. But once you practice, you'll find it extremely helpful. Also, remember that *outlines are extremely flexible.* The model above is popular, but you should modify it to fit your own purposes. Some writers, for example, don't distinguish between supporting points and details.

Like all writing processes, an outline benefits from revision. Your first time through, don't worry about getting all the ideas perfectly settled. In fact, you might even make adjustments during the writing process. Leave yourself room.

☞　　　　　☞　　　　　☞　　　　　☞

Brainstorming into Composing: Outlining in Action

Now it's your turn to write an outline. Using your brainstorming notes as reference, create a formal outline. (If you want to modify it, check your approach with your teacher first.) The outline should have at least three main topics.

Important: Since this is an exercise solely in outlining, feel free to invent supporting details for your main topics, as long as they're not too far-fetched. *However,* if you're going to compose an essay using this outline, your details must be factual.

The Thirty-Minute Essay

Why would anyone want to write an essay in thirty minutes? Is there any benefit in the exercise? What's the best approach?

Although writing a complete essay in thirty minutes is not easy, it is both possible and worthwhile. In fact, some assessment tests, including the SAT, now include *twenty*-minute essays. Certainly, you can't expect to do your best writing in half-an-hour; but the *pressure to compose* an essay quickly will help you refine your skills. In a sense, writing a thirty-minute essay is no different than writing a regular essay, only faster! Here are a few steps to follow.

- Organize your ideas. Define two or three main points within 5 minutes. Jot them down on the margin of your paper.

- Be sure to respond to the *question!* Be careful not to stray from the topic.

- Write your essay. Make your introduction interesting and use lots of supporting details to reinforce your main topic. Be sure to include a conclusion. The writing should take between 15–20 minutes.

- Proofread and then revise. Be especially careful to omit careless spelling and grammar mistakes. This should take 5-10 minutes.

Some students complain that they can't write *enough* in thirty minutes; that it takes them too long to articulate their ideas; or that they don't know what to write. That's why practicing thirty minute essays is valuable; the more you write them, the easier they become. However, keep in mind that *it's better to compose a brief, well-written essay than a longer, poorly written one*. And if you can't think of anything to say, begin *freewriting* what comes to your mind. Forget about being articulate or wise and just write!

Exercise

A) Write a thirty-minute essay. Your teacher will provide a topic. When you're done, exchange your essay with a classmate's. Offer each other constructive criticism.

In a few days, repeat this exercise.

Fiction

Creating a Main Character

In our next series of days, we will be building the framework for a story. Afterwards, you will have five days to write a first draft. We will begin with developing a main character.

Most beginning writers feel that plot is the most important element of fiction. While experienced writers would agree that a well-structured plot is essential to a good story, they would remind you that without thorough character development, even the best plots are dull. In fact, many fiction writers develop their main characters *before* deciding on a plot! The reason is simple: It's the *character* who defines the action. As an example, say you spend a day at the neighborhood mall and you get your wallet or purse stolen. In another town, the same happens to a student your age. Although the episodes are identical, the details of the story will be different *because of who you are!*

So, we will be dedicating a lot of time (and having fun!) developing a main character *before beginning a story.* Let's begin by making a list of basic character traits.

- gender
- age
- physical appearance
  - a. facial
  - b. weight
  - c. height
  - d. clothing or "image"
- religion
- economic status
- health

- family
  - a. siblings, including step-siblings
  - b. parents (married, divorced, etc.)
  - c. grandparents
- level of education
- employment
- hobbies
- experience of childhood

This list is only the beginning. Within each of these categories, there's room for countless details. And when you begin to describe personality, it gets really interesting! In fact, it's the idiosyncrasies that tell us the most about a character. Is he afraid of heights? Does she like sushi? Has there been some tragic or happy event that shaped his life? What does she think about all day?

Remember, these peculiarities reveal a character's inner life by *showing* us, not by *telling* us. Imagine reading about a character who, when crossing a street, "always stops mid-way, looks around, and then sprints the rest of the way." Isn't that more exciting than reading about a person who is "quite nervous when crossing streets"? So, you might want to include the following features to the ones listed above. *You should add as many as you like to the list!*

- superstitions
- physical peculiarities
- personal hygiene

- relationships
- favorite foods
- most embarrassing moment

Assignment

A) Spend two days creating a character. Beginning with the list of basic features, describe in *great detail* the main character of your story. Feel free to brainstorm more character traits. Gather as much information as you can. Include several idiosyncratic traits. Have fun!

Note: This exercise is meant to help you discover the richness and depth of your main character. Keep in mind, however, that when you write your story, *you'll want the character traits to surface sparingly.* The story will be bogged down if you describe too many character traits.

When you're done, *draw* your character on a posterboard. Be sure to include the character's name and a little bit of biographical information.

Main Character in a Mini-Mart:
Character Development in Action

Now it's time to bring your main character to life. By doing so, you'll see firsthand the importance of character development. Write a one-page episode describing what happens when your character buys groceries at the local mini-mart at 3:30 a.m. (Nothing spectacular has to take place! Just be sure to bring your character to life.)

Compare stories with your classmates'. Although all the characters went shopping at 3:30 a.m., what takes place is quite different. What takes place is determined by the character.

Setting

Setting is an essential element in fiction, inseparable from character and plot. Think about the influence of your own real-life setting. How much does the weather affect your choice of daily activities? Do you live in a rural or urban area? What are the streets like? Are they safe? Are computers part of your daily environment? Do you live in an area of ethnic diversity? Do you live in a house or an apartment? Is it quiet or noisy where you live?

Get the picture? The list of influences goes on. In a sense, you *are* your setting. The same is true for your main character.

In some cases, the setting is central to the plot, creating the action. Take this excerpt from Jack London's classic short story, "To Build a Fire."

> The man flung a look back along the way he had come. The Yukon lay a mile wide and hidden under three feet of ice. On top of this ice were as many feet of snow. It was all pure white, rolling in gentle undulations where the ice-jams of the freeze-up had formed.

Brrr! Clearly, the cold will play an important part in the man's journey.

Now, whether or not the setting is the primary focus, the key is to *keep it in the story*. Don't let the reader forget where and when the story is taking place. A careful writer will always weave the setting into the plot, embellishing the story with description. Remember, stories go stale when they are limited solely to plot and character.

Let's see firsthand how setting affects description. Study this description:

> -The waitress delivered our drinks. As the sun angled in the late-afternoon sky, we made a toast to the future. It felt good to be barefoot, sand on our feet, enjoying a vacation.

We can feel the couple's leisure and happiness. The setting sun and bare feet are linked to the mood of the scene. Compare it to the same scene with less attention to setting:

> -The waitress delivered our drinks. We made a toast to the future. We were enjoying our vacation.

Although we still feel the couple's happiness, the scene has little richness or depth. In fact, we don't know where the scene takes place. It could be anywhere.

Finally, setting often matches the emotion of the scene. How many movies have you seen when lightning and thunder begin just as the hero steps into a graveyard? How about lovers reuniting on the beach during sunset?

Assignment

A) With a small group, brainstorm a list of the influences of setting in your life. Remember that setting includes *time* as well as place! Include everything that comes to mind about your environment: population, air quality, temperature, wildlife, urban life, and so forth.

Now, create an original setting for your story, addressing the influences on your list. If you want your story to take place in *your* environment, continue with a more detailed description of the setting.

Weaving Setting Into an Episode

Once you've established your setting, it's time to practice incorporating it into your writing. Ask a classmate to volunteer a situation for your main character. The episode has to take place in the setting you created.

Write a one-page account of what happens, embellishing the action with descriptions of setting. Try to keep the action and the setting related.

Plot

Now that you've established a main character and a setting, you're ready to devise a *plot*. The plot is simply *what happens* in a story. Although there are many plots, they all share some common elements.

The heart of the plot is the *main conflict,* or the problem that motivates the action. Many students wonder if they *need* to have a conflict. The answer is yes! Think about it: Have you ever read a book or seen a movie when nothing goes wrong? When everything goes smoothly? Of course not. The plot is *generated* by the conflict.

Keep in mind that a main conflict can exist on a number of levels. It can come from within a character, such as a guilty conscience; it can exist between characters, such as a family battle; it can exist between a character and the outside world, such as a struggle for physical survival.

Most often, this conflict is established early in the story, even in the opening scene. Towards the middle of the plot comes the *climax,* when the conflict peaks. From then on the story moves towards *resolution.*

Of course, within the plot and resolution, any number of minor conflicts may arise. As you're writing, your main character will probably experience lots of setbacks. These are the events that enrich the plot, that make the story unique.

Let's take a firsthand look at these plot elements. We'll use "The Wizard of Oz" as our model.

- **Main conflict:** Dorothy wants to return to Kansas. This conflict propels her journey to Oz.

- **Climax:** Dorothy destroys the Wicked Witch of the West.

- **Resolution:** Dorothy clicks her heels together and returns home.

Although "The Wizard of Oz" is rich with lovable characters, humor and adventure, the plot is quite familiar: The main character is lost and journeys home. In fact, almost all plots are recycled. As we said earlier, plots are made interesting by the characters who fulfill them.

Assignment

A) Outline the plot of three of your favorite books. Find the main conflict, climax, and resolution.

Assignment

B) Many plots come directly from the life of the writer. In a small group, invent plots born of your own life experiences. Brainstorm minor events and details, adding fictitious elements if you like.

☞   ☞   ☞   ☞

Create a Plot

Devise a plot for your main character. Include main conflict, climax, resolution, and plot details.

Note: You might want to leave the resolution of the story undecided. If you would like to do this, clear your decision with your teacher.

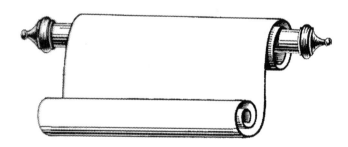

Dialogue

From the day we're born, dialogue is a part of our lives. As infants, we can't respond to our parents with words, so we express our feelings with tears and laughter. This exchange is our first experience of *dialogue,* a phenomenon that will continue throughout our lives. It makes sense, then, that dialogue is an essential element of a story. It brings the characters to life while adding believability to the story. Let's take a look at some of the important functions of dialogue.

First of all, dialogue gives a *voice* to your characters. This voice reflects personality, motivation, and upbringing. In short, dialogue helps describe a character. Compare the following examples:

- "Alas," said Mrs. Daly, "the rarefied air has weakened my spirits. I must return to the lowlands."
- "Dang," said Joey, "it ain't no good up here in this air. I gotta get home."

It's clear that Mrs. Daly and Joey have very different backgrounds. Mrs. Daly uses elevated language, while Joey relies on his hometown dialect. Take a moment to think about your own speaking voice. What does it reflect about your own background and personality?

This leads us to an important point: *Dialogue should reflect natural speech.* Normally, people speak in short sentences, using contractions and familiar expressions. Your characters should do the same. However, don't overdo it! Keep in mind that the dialogue has to be accessible and interesting.

Dialogue also serves to *advance the plot* of the story, offering a fresh alternative to narration. In mystery novels, for example, the plot often unfolds through dialogue instead of action. Notice how much we learn from this exchange:

"Where were you on the night of August 17th?" asked the detective.
"At the movies," answered Mr. Barlow. "What's it to you?"
"Some files were stolen from your office that night. Your partners have
reason to believe it was you."

Of course, dialogue shows more than action. We can also discover a character's feelings and motivations through conversation. Regardless of its purpose, always keep in mind that there should be a *reason* for the dialogue. A lingering conversation will weaken a story.

<u>Punctuating Dialogue</u>

Here are the rules to follow when punctuating dialogue:

- Put quotation marks around the *words being spoken.*
- Capitalize the first word of a direct quotation.
- Commas and end marks go *inside* the quotation marks.
- When the speaker changes, start a new paragraph.

Now see how each of the rules applies to the dialogue below:

"Well, well, well," said Grandpa Marty, "it's good to see you again."
"How many years has it been?" asked Samantha.
"Too many!" answered Grandpa.
Samantha smiled and said, "We have the whole summer to get acquainted."

Extension

There are a variety of ways to present direct quotes in a sentence. Sometimes, for example, a statement could be interrupted:

- "Meet me early," said Joanne, "so that we can go surfing."

Discuss other alternatives with your teacher.

Assignment

A) Using plenty of dialogue, write a one-page episode. Choose from one of the situations below, or make up your own. Be sure to follow the rules of punctuation.

- A soldier calls home to his wife.

- Three friends gossip about a new student.

- An employee resigns from work, explaining the reasons to his or her boss.

Point of View

Now that you've developed the main character, established the setting, and mapped out the plot, you must decide on the *point of view* you're going to use in your story. In other words, *who* is going to tell the story? The main character? A secondary character? A distant narrator? This is one of the most important choices you'll make. Imagine, for example, if *Jack and the Beanstalk* were told from the giant's point of view!

First Person

If you use *first person,* you participate in the story, using the pronoun *I* in the narration. Here is an example of first person point of view:

- I walked through the doorway and saw a magnificent garden.

In first person, the narrator's feelings and thoughts are on the surface, allowing for a great range of emotion and tone. The reader often feels personally attached to the storyteller. On the other hand, because the story is being told from one person's viewpoint, the overall scope of the narration is limited.

Third Person

A *third person* narrator tells a story without participating in it, using the pronouns *he, she, they,* and so forth, to tell the story. Here's the same sentence as above told in third person:

- She walked through the doorway and saw a magnificent garden.

Third person gives the narrator authority. He or she is free to move from character to character and from episode to episode. All "once upon a time" stories are told in third person.

If you use third person, you still have to choose between a *limited* or *omniscient* point of view. The omniscient (or "all knowing") narrator can relate any character's actions, thoughts, and emotions. The limited narrator is restricted to describing the action without delving into the inner lives of the characters. Here is an example of each third person point of view:

- Joey came up to bat with the bases loaded and two outs. In the stands, his dad sat nervously biting his nails. [limited]

- Joey tried to muster up some confidence as he came up to bat with the bases loaded and two outs. In the stands, his dad sat nervously biting his nails and remembering his own little league experiences. [omniscient]

Second Person

Second person is rarely used in narrative. It refers to the person being addressed, the *you* who is doing the reading. Second person is useful in interactive reading, like "create your own mystery" books and computer games. Here is an example:

- You walk through the doorway and see the magnificent garden. Do you enter?

☞   ☞   ☞   ☞

Practicing Point of View

Now it's time to practice different points of view. Using first person, make up a one page episode in your story.

The following day, describe the *same* episode from third person omniscient or third person limited point of view. This will introduce you to the advantages and disadvantages of each narrative strategy.

When you're done, decide which point of view best suits your story. Be prepared to justify your decision.

Drafting:
The Work Begins!

Now that you've set the groundwork for your story, you're ready to begin the first draft. It's time to *write!* This is where the real work begins, for even if you have original characters and a stirring plot, it's the writing that makes the story good.

Before beginning, you might want to review the earlier lessons on style, tone, parallelism, repetition, word choice, and so forth. After all, the demands of writing composition are the same for fiction: You must establish a consistent tone, a definite style and a consistent point of view. Keep the writing concise and rich with details.

In addition to the language itself, you should always be attentive to *how you are telling the story.* What types of writing will you use? When will you rely on description? Do you want to open with dialogue? When and how will you describe the main character(s)? Have you included enough setting? Here are a few tips for the structure of the story.

- Have a strong, clear opening: You want to interest the reader right away. Don't "warm up" the story. However, this doesn't mean that the opening has to be sensational.

- Develop the events clearly. Although you know the sequence of events, be sure that the reader does, too.

- Have a clear ending that leaves a strong impression on the reader. This doesn't mean you have to write a "happy" or "sad" ending. In fact, some stories end without the central conflict being resolved.

Now, although writing is very demanding, *your first draft should flow freely.* The first time through, you want the story to evolve naturally, leaving room for surprises. Don't be too concerned about perfecting the language. That will come during revision, when you're likely to exclude lots of the material.

<u>Note:</u> The only requirement for these five days is that you continue drafting your story. When you finish the first draft, begin revising. Try to complete a full draft of the story in five days.

Poetry

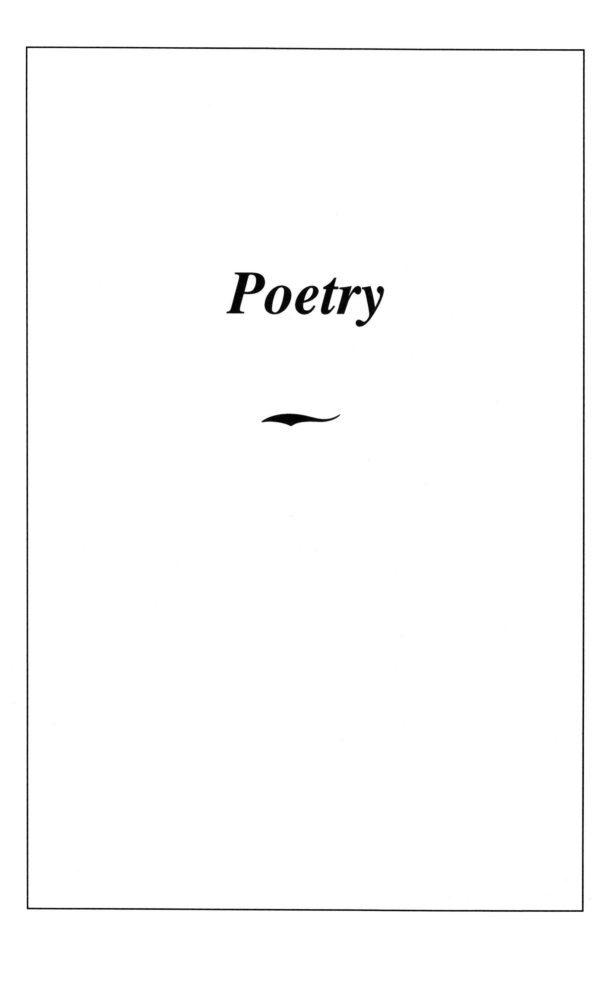

Writing Limericks:
An Introduction to Poetry

Before beginning

Before writing poetry, you should familiarize yourself with some useful terms. This will help you move through the different forms smoothly.

- First of all, when we speak about a poem's rhyming pattern, we refer to its *rhyme scheme*. This is signified by designating a different letter for each rhyme. Take, for example, the following lines from Edwin Arlington Robinson's, "Richard Cory."

> Whenever Richard Cory went down town, (A)
> We people on the pavement looked at him: (B)
> He was a gentleman from sole to crown, (A)
> Clean favored, and imperially slim. (B)

  If another rhyme is introduced, it would be signified by the letter 'C.'

- We will also refer to line length, or the amount of *syllables per line*. Many fixed-forms contain ten syllables per line, while the amount varies in others.

- *Stanzas* are the units of lines in the poem. They are like paragraphs.

Limericks

More than any other form of poetry, *limericks* lend themselves to humor. The rhyme scheme and line length create a cadence that's easy to follow and fun to write. Read the following limerick aloud. Does the form seem familiar? Do you notice the cadence?

> There once was a man from Mars (A)
> Who owned three thousand cars. (A)
>   He wanted five more, (B)
>   But when he drove to the store (B)
> He lost his cars in the stars. (A)

The rhyme scheme is simple: *a, a, b, b, a.* Lines 1, 2, and 5 have about the same number of syllables, usually between 7 and 9. Lines 3 and 4 are shorter, usually between 5-7 syllables.

Assignment

A) Write three limericks. Read them to your classmates.

Extension

Group limericks are very entertaining. Simply pass a piece of paper around, taking turns adding lines to a limerick.

Writing Haiku:
The Art of Imagery

You might be familiar with *haiku*, a form of poetry which originated in Japan during the 15th century. It began as a 17-syllable verse, or stanza, but soon became a poem in itself. Most often, haiku is a celebration of nature. Still popular among poets, haiku is concise, combining *imagery* to produce emotion and meaning. An *image* is a picture in words. Although images are usually related to sight, they can include all the senses: smell, taste, sound and touch.

Importantly, a vivid image appeals to both the senses *and the emotions*. Haiku depends upon the image to provide this depth. Always remember that the image does much more than decorate a poem—it should enhance the poem's meaning.

Here are the structural features of the 17 syllable haiku: a) it has 3 lines, b) the first and third lines have 5 syllables, c) the second line has 7 syllables. Here's an example:

> The light rising fast (5)
> Over the far eastern plains (7)
> Brings daytime to all. (5)

Assignment

A) Now it's time for you to practice this ancient form. Write three haiku. Be sure to create vivid images. Feel free to adorn your poems with drawings.

Writing a Sonnet

The *Sonnet* is a more challenging form than the two previous ones. When it originated in 13th century Italy, it referred to any short poem. Since that time, the sonnet has acquired several fixed-forms. It is among the most treasured forms, a common vehicle of love poetry. Let's take a look at an English, or Shakespearean, sonnet. Here are its features:

- Like most sonnet forms, the English sonnet contains 14 lines.
- It has ten syllables per line.
- It is one stanza.
- Note the rhyme scheme below. The final two lines are called a *couplet*, or pair of rhyming lines.

Sonnet LXXIII

That time of year thou mayst in me behold(A)
When yellow leaves, or none, or few, do hang (B)
Upon those boughs which shake against the cold, (A)
Bare ruined choirs, where late the sweet birds sang; (B)
In me thou see'st the twilight of such day (C)
As after the sunset fadeth in the west, (D)
Which by and by black night doth take away, (C)
Death's second self, that seals up all in rest. (D)
In me thou see'st the glowing of such fire (E)
That on the ashes of his youth doth lie, (F)
As the death-bed whereon it must expire, (E)
Consumed with that which it was nourished by. (F)
This thou perceiv'st, which makes thy love more strong, (G)
To love that well which thou must leave ere long. (G)

—William Shakespeare

Assignment

A) Now it's time to compose your own English sonnet. Although you'll probably find the form challenging, keep at it. The struggle will pay off! Before beginning, here are some helpful hints:

- Unless you have a good reason to do otherwise, use your *natural* vocabulary when writing poetry. Some students have the tendency to sound old-fashioned when writing verse.

- Instead of struggling to find ten syllable lines and a perfect rhyme scheme, write a first draft, and then work with your lines.

Extension

Read a *Spenserian* sonnet and an *Italian* sonnet. Learn the form of each and compose sonnets accordingly.

Free Verse

So far, we've been writing fixed-form poems, verses that are regulated by syllable count or rhyme scheme. Now it's time to break away and enter the world of free verse.

Free verse simply means that the poem does not have a pre-set form. However, this doesn't mean that you can write *anything*! Instead, *you're responsible for finding a form that suits your poem's spirit and meaning.* This responsibility makes free verse very demanding.

Let's take a look at a poet's use of free verse. Walt Whitman, one of America's greatest poets, celebrated life. He was a free spirit who didn't want to leave *anything* out of his poetry. Thus, he needed a form that could absorb his intention. Here is an excerpt from "There was a Child Went Forth." Read it out loud.

> The early lilacs became part of this child,
> And grass and white and red morning-glories, and white and red clover,
>   and the song of the phoebe-bird,
> And the Third-month lambs and the sow's pink-faint litter, and mare's foal
>   and the cow's calf,
> And the noisy brood of the barnyard or by the mire of the pondside,
> And the fish suspending themselves so curiously below there, and the
>   beautiful curious liquid,
> And the water-plants with their graceful flat heads, all became part of him.

Notice the rhythm that Whitman establishes. The long lines, with their catalogue of objects, have a kind of prayerful cadence that makes the poem feel vast. Imagine if these lines were regulated to ten syllables and a rhyme scheme. Wouldn't the meaning of the poem suffer? However, another free verse poem might beg for shorter lines and shorter stanzas. This depends on the tone and content of the poem.

Assignment

A) Compose a free verse poem. You might want to write the poem first, and then decide on the form. But before deciding on your style, ask yourself the following questions:

- What's the tone of my poem?
- What's my poem about?
- How long should the lines be?
- How long should the stanzas be?

When you're done, read your poem to the class. Be prepared to explain your free verse style.

Line Break

Most beginning poets don't consider the importance of *line breaks* in their work. Line break is a term that stands for *where the line ends.* In fixed forms such as sonnets, line break is determined by syllable count. In free verse, however, the poet must decide the best place to break the line.

But does line break really matter? How does it affect the meaning of the poem? Study the following versions of the same stanza. Can you see how the different line breaks affect the meaning of each?

> I can see the bull staring at me
> through the diamond spaces of the fence.

> I can see the bull
> staring at me
> through the diamond spaces
> of the fence.

> I can see the bull staring
> at me
> through the diamond spaces of the fence.

Got it? In the first stanza, we don't know where the bull is until the second line. In the second stanza, the information unfolds more slowly, creating tension and suspense. (Also notice how the third line ends with *spaces,* leaving a wide-open feeling.) The final stanza is rather humorous (or dramatic) when the two words *at me* have the weight of their own line. Clearly, line breaks affect the meaning of the stanza.

Although being attentive to line break is important, be careful not to become overly concerned. You should always write your poem first, and then consider the line break.

Assignment

A) This is a three-part assignment. First, write a free verse poem. Be sure to pay attention to line break. Next, redo the poem with different line breaks. Finally, on a separate sheet of paper, explain how the changes in line breaks affected the meaning of the poem.

Writing Blank Verse

One of the most common forms of poetry is *blank verse*. Poems written in blank verse contain ten syllables per line, but the lines do not rhyme. There are no regulations for stanza size or the length of the poem. A great deal of Shakespeare's work is written in blank verse, as is Milton's *Paradise Lost.*

Of all the poetic forms, blank verse is closest to natural speech. Let's see if this quality surfaces in this excerpt from Robert Frost's famous poem, "Mending Wall."

> Something there is that doesn't love a wall,
> That sends the frozen-ground swell under it
> And spills the upper boulders in the sun,
> And makes gaps even two can pass abreast.
> The work of hunters is another thing:
> I have come after them and made repair
> Where they have left not one stone on a stone,
> But they would have the rabbit out of hiding.

Notice the ten-syllable, non-rhyming lines. Do they have a natural flow to them? What kind of freedom does the release from rhyming allow?

Assignment

A) Write a blank verse poem at least sixteen lines long. You might want to write the poem first, and then make the necessary adjustments to create ten-syllable lines.

Writing Song Lyrics

Have you ever written a song? Have you ever wondered who writes the *lyrics,* or words, to your favorite songs? You'd be surprised to discover how many singers don't write their own lyrics. Often, they hire poets or other songwriters to write the words. Why? Because composing good song lyrics is very challenging. Like poetry, lyric writing demands precision and grace.

One of the obvious challenges in lyric writing is *matching the words to the music.* If the music is dark and mysterious, for example, the lyrics shouldn't be upbeat. Furthermore, song lyrics, like poems, have structure. Normally, they are broken into *verses* interrupted by a *chorus* that repeats several times. Also, song lyrics almost always employ a rhyme scheme. The most common ones include *a, b, a, b,* or *a, a, b, a,* or *a, b, c, b.* Notice the rhyme scheme and chorus of "America the Beautiful."

> Oh beautiful for spacious skies (A)
> For amber waves of grain (B)
> For purple mountain's majesty (A)
> Upon the fruited plains. (B)
>
> CHORUS
> America, America, (A)
> God shed His grace on thee, (B)
> And crown thy good with brotherhood (C)
> From sea to shining sea. (B)

Although the above rhyme schemes are still common, popular songs changed drastically with the Beatles. By changing meter, time signature, key and form within the same song, they broke with traditional lyric schemes. Now, we have few if any rules left as to how to write a good lyric. Think about your favorite Rap or Punk song. What kind of rhyme scheme does it follow?

One way to test the quality of lyrics is to *read* them apart from the music. Do they convey a meaning? Do they move you? Hopefully, the lyrics can stand alone and still be considered a work of art. Unfortunately, the quality of lyrics doesn't seem to matter to some artists: As long as the song has a good melody and a good beat, everything is okay! How many songs have you heard with lyrics like these?

> Oh, my sweet sweetheart
> Let me show you how much I love you.
> Please don't tell me maybe.
> There's no one else above you.

Do these lines sound familiar? You'll probably agree that they are rather shallow and uninventive. Sadly enough, lyrics like these can be heard in lots of hit songs.

Assignment

A) Bring a tape of your favorite song, along with the lyrics, to your class. Read the lyrics out loud. After explaining the structure of the song (rhyme scheme, verses, and chorus) tell the class why you find the lyrics meaningful. What makes them good?

Next, play the song to the class.

Note: You might want to have someone make a song collection consisting of everyone's favorites. It's a terrific souvenir!

Assignment

B) Write song lyrics. Be sure to have *at least* four verses and a chorus. Establish a consistent rhyme scheme. (If you feel adventurous, try setting the lyrics to music.)

When you're done, read your lyrics to the class.

Group Poem

Whether you try it in the classroom or at a party, this next activity is lots of fun.

Get in a group of five or six people. The first person writes the title and the first four lines of a poem. Then she folds the paper over, leaving *only the last line visible.*

The next person reads this line and continues the poem, adding four lines and then leaving one visible. This process continues until the final person writes four lines and an ending.

When you're all done, read the poem out loud. You'll be amazed at the twists and turns!

Writing a Sestina:
The Final Challenge!

The *sestina* is one of the most challenging forms of poetry, but also one of the most innovative. Invented in the 12th century, it is even older than the sonnet. Rather than rhyming, the sestina repeats a series of six words, one at the end of each line. Each stanza contains these same words in a different order.

For example, say you're writing a sestina about the beach. You use the end-words *sand, wave, sun, shell, seaweed,* and *beach* in your first stanza:

> The gentle white sand
> disappears under the wave
> as it splashes. The sun
> has yet to break through the shell
> of fog. I grab a handful of seaweed
> and run with it along the beach.

Let's number each of the end-words: *sand* is 1, *wave* is 2, *sun* is 3, *shell* is 4, *seaweed* is 5, and *beach* is 6. The next five stanzas contain the same end-words, only in a different order. The second stanza goes 6,1,5,2,4,3. It might read something like this:

> After a while, the beach
> gets crowded. People are kicking sand
> on our towels. I want to tie them up in seaweed
> for doing that! Suddenly, the waves
> grow bigger, so I put my special shell
> under my towel to keep it away from the sun.

Got it? Here are the structures of the first six stanzas:

1	6	3	5	4	2
2	1	6	3	5	4
3	5	4	2	1	6
4	2	1	6	3	5
5	4	2	1	6	3
6	3	5	4	2	1

The seventh stanza is a little different. It has only three lines, each of which uses two of the end-words in their original order. For example, the final stanza of our beach sestina might sound like this:

I wipe the sand from my feet and hear the roar of the waves.
The sun is sinking, but I still have the lucky shell
I found in the seaweed during our day at the beach.

By now you can tell that there's a lot of *play* involved in a sestina. Using the same words over and over again and trying to sound natural takes a lot of inventiveness!

Assignment

A) Take two days to write a sestina. Be sure to follow the structure. **Hint**: Nouns are the most accommodating end-words, since they can be used in lots of different ways. This is especially true for nouns that can be made into verbs, like *pile, picture,* or *dress.*

Note: Traditionally, the lines of a sestina are ten syllables long. However, for our purposes we have simplified the form. Feel free to use the traditional form if you like.

Writing in Action

Writing a Business Letter

Letter writing is one of the most valuable writing skills you can acquire. Whether you're writing to a friend, a business, a politician, or an editor, a competent letter will produce results. Bad letter writing, on the other hand, can interfere with your intentions, especially in a business letter.

The most important aspect of any letter is, of course, the *writing.* If you write a letter marred with grammar errors and misspellings, it's going to be ineffective. But if your sentences are fluid, your tone appropriate, and your message clear, the letter will be convincing. *There's no replacement for good writing.*

Different letters require different forms and writing styles. Following these forms is essential. For example, if you write a friendly letter to a business, they're likely to dismiss your correspondence as unprofessional.

Let's begin with the business letter, which includes six parts. Study this sample business letter. Notice the placement of each of the six parts. This is called the *semiblock form.*

Heading   Joanne Doe
1875 Grand Ave
New York, NY 10010
January 14, 1995

Inside Address
Mr. Eli Smith
Cleaning Incorporated
238 Main Street
Barnville, MA 01002

Salutation
Dear Mr. Smith:

Body
I am writing to inquire about your carpet cleaner. A few days ago, I went shopping. To my disappointment, I discovered that your carpet cleaner was not in stock. The store manager said the cleaner was unavailable.

Could you kindly let me know if you intend to reintroduce the product? I find it the most effective cleaner on the market. I would be disappointed if you dropped it from your production line.

With thanks for your time.

Closing   Sincerely,

Signature   Joanne Doe
Joanne Doe

Here are the six parts of the business letter. Note their placement in the letter above.

- **Heading:** Includes your name, address, and the date.

- **Inside address:** Includes the address of the recipient. Use the person's name if you know it.

- **Salutation:** Greets the recipient. Use *Mr., Ms., Mrs.,* and so forth. If you don't know the person's name, use *Dear Sir or Madam.*

- **Body:** Conveys the message of the letter.

- **Closing:** Ends the letter. There are several options, including *Yours truly* and *Sincerely.*

- **Signature:** Sign the letter in ink. Below the signature, type your full name.

Notice the tone of the letter. The writer is both *direct* and *respectful.* Although she is not chummy, she keeps an amiable tone.

Note: Some people prefer the *block form* of the business letter, which sets the heading directly above the inside address.

Assignment

A) Write a business letter. Try to write one that you'll send! Be careful to follow the correct form and to write carefully, with an appropriate tone.

Here are some common topics for business letters. Choose one, or make up your own.

- Letter of complaint
- Letter trying to negotiate a deal
- Letter refusing payment
- Letter asking for payment
- Letter of satisfaction/dissatisfaction

Writing a Friendly Letter

When you're writing a friend, you probably don't consider the form of your letter—and rightly so. After all, your friend won't be offended if your letter lacks a heading! On the other hand, the friendly letter has a standard form that is useful in many cases. Look at the following list. The friendly letter should be applied for these occasions.

- Thank you letters
- Accepting/declining invitations
- Birth announcements
- Notes of congratulations or sorrow
- School notes/excuses

Let's look at a sample friendly letter. The parts are labeled.

Heading   1875 Grand Ave
                New York, NY 10010
                January 14, 1995

Salutation
Dear Mr. and Mrs. Donnelley,

   Body
   Thanks so much for the invitation to your anniversary party this summer, but I'm afraid we'll be unable to attend.
   The kids have soccer camp, and Marie is busy finishing up her degree. On top of that, I just got a big project with a strict deadline. A trip to California would simply be impossible. I'm sure you understand.
   Thanks again for your kind invitation. Hopefully, we can visit in the near future. Congratulations on your anniversary!

               Closing Love,

               Signature Joanne

This letter has a personal, light tone. The writer is able to graciously decline the invitation without sounding self-conscious. Just as you don't want to sound too familiar in a business letter, you don't want to come across as businesslike in a personal letter. It's all about *tone!*

The form is simpler than that of the business letter. Note the absence of both the inside address and the typewritten signature. Also, the salutation is followed by a comma instead of a colon. Finally, it's preferable to hand write personal letters in *ink*. Never use pencil!

Assignment

A) Choose one of the occasions listed above as a subject for a friendly letter. Be sure to follow the correct form and to write carefully, with an appropriate tone.

Writing a Speech

Speech making is an important part of the working world. Whether you're a principal, a politician, a student, a celebrity, or a lawyer, at one time or another you'll need to make a speech. And like so many presentation skills, speeches depend on *good writing*. A poorly written speech won't move an audience, even if the presenter is an excellent speaker.

Let's take a look at two different kinds of speeches, beginning with the *expository* speech. Expository writing gives *information*. Suppose you report on the impact of funding in education. After gathering research, you deliver an expository speech presenting your information. However, you *don't take sides*. Expository speeches can be quite fascinating, especially when they deliver two sides of an issue. An informative speech on UFO's, for example, provides the listener with lots of facts and theories on *both* sides.

A *persuasive* speech, on the other hand, is an attempt to convince listeners of one point of view. Politicians constantly deliver persuasive speeches, trying to win over their audience. Lawyers, too, rely on persuasion to convince judge and jury. However, in both cases (especially the politician's) writers often compose the speeches.

So, what are the elements of a well-written speech? What should you consider when composing a speech?

It's no surprise that a good speech and a good essay share many of the same features. In opening a speech, you want to hook your listener right away. In developing a speech, you should rely on supporting details. The speech should be well-structured and the writing should be mechanically sound.

However, remember that there's a difference between written and spoken English. Since a speech is meant to be spoken, it has to *sound* good. Don't use obscure words or sentences that are so complex they're hard to follow. Also, be sure to practice reading the speech out loud many times. Try to tape record it; this will give you an idea if it's "listener friendly."

Before writing a speech, keep the following things in mind:

- *Know your audience:* Have you ever been at a graduation when a guest of honor gives a long oration about himself? Meanwhile, this speaker's life is the last thing on the graduates' minds! But since a speech is appropriate for such an occasion, the speaker should at least choose a topic that will interest his audience. (A speech about employment opportunities, for example.) So, always keep your audience in mind.

- *Limit the topic:* Like good essays, good speeches must remain focused. If you drift into tangents, you'll lose your audience. Also, know how long the speech is supposed to be *before* writing it. Don't write an hour-long speech for a twenty-minute presentation!

- Be sure to use the *appropriate tone and language* for the audience. If you're speaking at a business meeting, for example, you don't want to use informal language!

Assignment

A) Use the next three days to compose a speech, either persuasive or expository. Be sure to follow all the pointers given above, and to practice reciting it *many times.*

Extension

Deliver your speech to your class. Here are a few tips you might find helpful:

- Be sure to *project* and *enunciate*. The entire audience must be able to hear you and understand you clearly.

- Stand confidently and keep your body *controlled*. Although arm motions are acceptable and even necessary, beware of the temptation to sway or to lean during a speech. (You might even find yourself playing with your hair or scratching your head.) Be sure to iron out these nervous reactions before making your speech.

- Make *eye contact*. This is essential in establishing both intimacy and authority. Be sure to make eye contact with a wide section of the audience.

Reporting a News Event:
An Introduction to Journalism

Every day, thousands of newspapers and magazines are printed around the world. Each of these publications contains a host of articles. With that much reporting going on, every writing student should know what it takes to write good journalism. Let's begin with reporting a news event.

When reporting an event, the journalist remains *objective*. In other words, she simply explains the facts. In contrast to essay writing and creative writing, your opinion is not appropriate in a news report. If you're writing about a conflict, you should present all sides of a story, giving equal space and emphasis to each. In order to keep to the facts, reporters ask themselves six questions. These questions cover the basics, ensuring objectivity and thoroughness in the reporting. They are usually answered in the *first paragraph* of the article. Here they are:

WHO?   WHAT?   WHEN?   WHERE?   WHY?   HOW?

Once these questions are answered, the rest of the article provides details, from most to least important. Try an experiment. Read a front page article. Can you identify the answer to the journalist's questions? Now notice the writer's style and tone. Like all writers, journalists must write well. In general, reporters keep their style and tone direct. This is especially true when reporting news events. It's the *news* that's important; the writing shouldn't call attention to itself.

Of course, there are exceptions to this rule. Editorials, columns, and reviews are often full of flare and personality. We'll take a look at these shortly.

Assignment

A) Referring to the journalist's standard questions, write an article about a real or fictitious news event. The event can be local, national, or international.

Note: Be sure to follow the correct form of the news article. Include a *title*, and write the location of the event first, in capital letters. It might look something like this:

Brush Fire Rages On

LOS ANGELES—A massive brush fire continues to rage....

Writing an Editorial

Besides reporting the news, periodicals and newspapers also have *editorials.* Editorials are articles that express a writer's opinions. Keep in mind that the editorials normally don't reflect the beliefs of the publication, but of the author. A strong editorial will move its readers, whether they agree with the article or not. Thankfully, most publications print letters from the readers, which are editorials in their own right.

So, what makes an editorial effective? How does it differ from a news article? Let's look at some of the elements of good editorials.

First, unlike news articles, editorials express viewpoints. The tone of the writing, therefore, is vital to its success. You should come across as secure and authoritative, without appearing overconfident or arrogant. Besides that, editorials express all kinds of sentiments: humor, outrage, sadness, gratitude, and so forth.

Second, like all forms of writing, it's the *supporting details* that convince the reader. Statistics, direct quotes, and real-life examples are valuable tools in persuasion. Remember, without a well-structured argument, even the most charming editorial will be unconvincing. Be sure to use effective transitions and solid mechanics. This is where your writing skills pay off.

Third, keep to the point! Because editorials are heartfelt, it's easy to stray from the topic. If you're writing about the importance of art in education, for example, you might want to describe a third grade field trip to a museum. However, we don't need to hear about every statue or work of art.

Assignment

A) Read a published editorial. What is the tone? Is it well-structured? Is it convincing? Does it remain focused?

Assignment

B) Write an editorial about a contemporary issue. When you're done, read it to the class.

Conducting an Interview

Have you ever bought a magazine because it included an interview with one of your heroes? Have you ever needed to find information through an interview? Certainly, interviews serve an important role in journalism, providing an angle that the news article cannot. Learning the art of interviewing, therefore, is a valuable skill for any writer. But what makes interviews so useful?

First of all, interviews provide *firsthand* information. If a celebrity is speaking about his life, the news is direct—there's no room for interpretation. The same applies for experts, whose knowledge is often used to support an argument. Secondly, interviews are appealing because they are *personal*. Good interviews have a sense of intimacy that draws the reader in. We *want* to know about our politicians, celebrities, artists, athletes and scientists.

Now, what makes an interview interesting? How does one go about preparing an interview? Here are a few things to remember when conducting an interview.

To begin with, decide on the questions *before* doing the interview. This will help you remain relaxed and focused. Of course, questions will arise spontaneously in the conversation, so be prepared! Be sure to ask questions that will inspire discussion and explanation. You want the person to *express* herself. Avoid 'yes' or 'no' questions. Order your questions from most to least important. You don't know how much talking your guest will do, so get to the essential material first.

Preferably, tape record the interview. Otherwise, jot down the key facts. Don't get lost in the writing; that will come later.

Usually, the interviewer is an objective reporter. Don't make value judgments about the person's responses. Remember, your job is to ask informed questions and put them into writing, a process which takes a great deal of discrimination. Because the interview should be both informative and appealing, exclude the material that's weighty or repetitious. However, be sure to include all *important* information. Finally, always begin with some biographical information about the person you're interviewing.

Assignment

A) Read a published interview. Is it interesting? Are the questions informative? Do they inspire conversation and explanation? Are you more interested in the person being interviewed after your reading? Did you learn something about the topic of the interview?

Assignment

B) Write a list of questions, then conduct an interview. Now write the interview, editing when it's necessary. Share the interview with your classmates.

Writing a Review

Have you ever wondered whether or not a movie or play is worth seeing? Most people have. One way to find out is to read *reviews,* which appear in most periodicals. Whether the subject is literature, theater, film, dance, or art, reviews serve two basic functions: summary and opinion. A book review, for example, would present the plot of the book (without giving away the ending!), along with the reviewer's opinion. Thorough book reviews go into such matters as character development, writing style, theme, and so forth.

This general approach applies to other kinds of reviews, but each subject requires attention to different details. If you were reviewing a play, for instance, you would want to attend to the actors as well as the playwright. A film requires attention to soundtrack and cinematography.

Like editorials, reviews don't express the opinion of the publication as a whole; however, the editors must decide how much leeway to give the writers. While most reviewers maintain a straightforward tone, some are forceful or even eccentric.

Because readers turn to reviews for advice, reviewers should provide good *reasons* for their opinions. After all, the article is about the movie, not the writer! So, don't write, "The movie was great" without explaining why. Was the acting superb? Was it suspenseful?

Assignment

A) Read a published review. Study its form. Does it provide a summary? Does the reviewer give reasons for his opinion? Describe the tone of the review. (You might find it easiest to look in Sunday editions of newspapers and in weekly magazines.)

Assignment

B) Write a thorough review about a book, movie, or play. When you're done, read it to the class.

Note: Some reviewers rely on gimmicks, such as scales from 1-10, or thumbs-up and thumbs-down. Feel free to devise your own gimmick, but don't let it substitute for writing.

Writing a Column

Most journalists would love to have a *column*. A column is an article that is featured regularly, either daily or weekly. Not only does a column ensure lots of exposure, but it allows the writer to develop her own voice and personality while building a loyal readership.

There are many kinds of columns: Sports writers give insights on athletes and teams; psychologists answer letters and give advice; cooks share their favorite recipes; political analysts tell us what to expect in the coming election. The list goes on. Although the content and form of these columns differ, they all share certain features.

First of all, a columnist must be an expert on his subject. With so much exposure, his authority is always up to question. Of course, this doesn't apply when the column is more *subjective*, or based on opinion. Nevertheless, the writing should maintain a sense of authority.

Furthermore, a columnist must be a competent writer. Even if he is an authority on his subject, if he can't write well, his column won't be interesting. Again, *there's no substitute for good writing.*

Finally, a columnist must have some kind of *appeal;* after all, she depends on loyal readers. This appeal is related to lots of things: content, writing style, personality and outlook, to name a few. Often, the writer will be humorous or biting, controversial or heartwarming.

Assignment

A) Read a columnist who interests you. Study his writing style. Is the person an expert? Why do you think readers find him appealing?

Assignment

B) Suppose you want to submit your own weekly column to an editor. Considering your interests, write an article that demonstrates your expertise and your appeal. Remember, you're trying to convince the editor that you can *sustain* a column over a long period of time.

Writing an Advertisement

In today's society, there's almost no way to escape the onslaught of advertising. During a typical day, we see commercials on TV, read billboards as we drive, get direct mail (or "junk mail") at home, and read ads in periodicals.

Writers play an important role in advertising. Although some ads are purely visual, most rely on skilled writing to be effective. And since advertisers have limited space, each word must count. So, what are the strategies of an effective ad? What does a writer consider when composing an ad?

First of all, the ad, whether a full page or a few sentences, must *hook the reader*. This hook is often visual, but it should be accompanied by a catchy phrase or headline. (People *do* judge books by their covers!) Which headline interests you more: "Drink Barney's Soda Every Day," or "Tickle Your Day With Barney's Soda"?

Once the reader is involved, you need to convince him that he should purchase the product. More specifically, you must convince him that buying the product will improve his *quality of life*. The longer the ad, the more room you have to convince the reader. Here's a brief example:

> "Having a rough day? Has the work week got you down? No problem! Let Barney's Soda tickle you back into action! One sip and you'll be smiling!"

In addition to engaging the reader's emotions, you also want to assure him that the product is of high quality; he needs to know that he's making a good decision. (Notice how much merchandise is "new and improved," or "half the cost of the leading product.") This is done by using powerful language and a confident tone:

> "We're so sure you'll be pleased with Barney's Soda, we GUARANTEE IT! If you aren't satisfied with Barney's unique taste and energizing ingredients, simply mail us a letter, along with proof of purchase, and we'll refund your money, no questions asked!"

Finally, an effective ad compels the reader to act *now*:

> "So, what are you waiting for? Are you going to let another day wind down? Quench your thirst and boost your day with Barney's Soda!"

Assignment

A) Gather several different types of ads, including direct mail, newspaper and magazine ads. Discuss their qualities. Are they effective? Why or why not? How do they differ?

Assignment

B) Write two advertisements. Choose among a magazine ad, a newspaper ad, and a direct mail letter. *Don't* do a TV commercial—that's next. Be sure to include all the elements listed above. If you like, include a photo in your ad.

Writing a Television Commercial

Millions of people watch television every day. In fact, many of us get our ideas about the world *through* television. It makes sense, then, that companies want to advertise their products on TV. What other medium can guarantee millions of viewers? This exposure leads companies to invest *enormous* amounts of money and time into commercials. They know it's the commercial—not the product—that hooks the viewer. You may have a quality product, but if consumers don't know about it, or it's not presented well, it will lose sales.

Successful commercials have two things in common: They *attract viewers* and they *sell a product*. In a 15-30 second ad, there's no room for boredom or empty time! But what makes a commercial appealing and effective? Although good commercials come in many forms, most fit into the following groups. Each group appeals to a different emotion. And in each case, the ad promises the viewer a better quality of life *if* she purchases the product.

The *sentimental* ad touches our hearts. Here's a familiar scenario: A boy strikes out in a baseball game. His parents give him a hug and then they all drive to a fast food restaurant. As the boy takes a bite of his hamburger, a smile comes across his face, and his sorrow is gone!

The *fashionable* commercial appeals to our desire to be "high class." Car commercials often depict a wealthy couple driving along a beautiful shoreline, and then pulling into the long driveway of their mansion. Meanwhile, the narrator explains why the car is a model of perfect engineering.

Humorous ads hook the viewers by making them laugh: A father guzzles down his kid's drink because it is so delicious. A flock of sheep rush to a carpet sale....

Finally, some commercials try to appeal to the *consumer* in us. These commercials use "real life" comparisons and statistics, including taste tests, price wars, letters from customers, and so on. They also rely on endorsements, which come from doctors, athletes, and celebrities, among others.

Keep in mind that each of these sentiments is appropriate for certain products and a certain audience. You don't want to appeal to a sense of fashion in order to sell popcorn, just as humor won't go a long way in selling a luxury automobile!

Assignment

A) Watch three television commercials. Try to discover the main sentiment in each. What audience is each one aimed at? Write down your observations and share them with the class.

Assignment

B) In a group of two or three, write a 30-second television commercial. Include all the dialogue and the descriptions of events. Imagine your group is handing the commercial straight to the director for filming. When you're done, act out your commercial in front of the class.

Keeping a Diary

No matter where you go, you will find people writing in their diaries. You might be keeping one yourself. In fact, the *diary* (or journal) is probably the most universal of all writing forms, crossing lines of history, language and culture. Why is this? Why do people write diaries?

To begin with, you don't need to be a writer to keep a diary; there are no rules—it's just you and your feelings. Also, journal writing is *fun,* no matter what your age. After all, what's more fascinating to you than your own life? But most importantly, diaries allow you to express yourself, to get in touch with your feelings while keeping your personal history. This is why journal writing is so good for you.

As you grow older, diaries become priceless memoirs. Imagine being seventy-five years old and reading from a journal you wrote when you were sixteen!

Assignment

A) Spend forty-five minutes today writing a diary entry. If you already have a journal, simply add to it. Be sure to record the date on your entry.

Write a Letter to Yourself and Receive it in a Year

Here is a unique and intimate way to experience journal writing. The procedure is simple: Compose a letter to yourself, seal it in an envelope with an address that will be good in a *year*. Give the letter to your teacher, who will mail it in 365 days!

It's best to write your letter in solitude and in a natural setting. Take time to reflect. Of course, there are no rules or standards to follow in your letter. It's personal and confidential, so write freely.

When you begin the letter, remember that you'll be a year older when you receive it. What do you want to say to your future self? Do you want to reflect on your life now? Do you want to make some goals for yourself? Is there an inspiring thought that you want to hold?

Give time and sincerity to this assignment. After all, you're giving it to yourself.

Fiction and the Diary

Real-life diaries are fascinating. Many famous ones remain, captivating us with their intimacy.   It's no wonder, then, that lots of fiction appears in diary form. They reveal a character's private thoughts; and we get to see the world, day-by-day, through another's eyes. Furthermore, the diary entries structure the story, mirroring the daily rhythms of life.

Like any type of writing, the diary has its challenges, especially in fiction. Creating well-rounded characters and a well-structured plot, for instance, can be difficult. It's also harder to weave setting and dialogue into diary entries. Nevertheless, you should try to include these elements in order to enrich your story.

Don't forget that *you have to write well!* (In this assignment, lots of students overlook this.) An imaginary diary, unlike a personal diary, has to be engaging *for the reader.*   This does not mean that you have to follow Standard English, of course; after all, most people use dialect in their journals.

Assignment

A) In the next two days, write a story in diary form. Include at least four thorough diary entries.

Writing an Epistolary Scene

If you've ever corresponded with a friend for a long time, you know how revealing letters can be. Like diaries, they are the record keepers of our lives. But unlike diaries, they are written *to* another person. Letters, therefore, involve a *relationship*, making them a wonderful medium for fiction.

'Epistle' simply means "a letter." So, *epistolary* literature is written in the form of a correspondence between two or more people. You're probably already imagining the wonderful possibilities! It can be lots of fun! However, like the fictitious diary, telling a complete story in this form is not easy. Here are some things to keep in mind.

Be sure to develop each character's distinct voice, and don't deviate from it! Since you can't describe the character in a traditional narrative, the person has to come to life through the *tone and style* of writing. This is where your sensitivity to tone pays off.

Keep in mind that the plot has to unfold through the letters. Each correspondence should further the plot. How fast the plot develops depends on the length of the epistolary. Keep the reader involved by leaving questions unanswered. You don't want every letter to be a dramatic confession!

In the early letters, be sure to give the necessary background to the story. How do the characters know one another? Are they pen pals who never met? Did they fall in love on a cruise long ago? Also, keep in mind that even though the characters are corresponding, they can meet in the course of the story.

Assignment

A) In the next two days, write an epistolary story that's at least six letters long. Remember to have your characters date and sign the letters.

Technical Writing

In the near future, computers will be as common as telephones. Already we live in a world where "fax machine," "e-mail," and "modem" are everyday words. This technological revolution has brought with it a new wave in writing: *technical writing.*

Technical writers serve lots of needs, but their most important task is *translating technology to ordinary people.* With the rate of technological advance, the need for technical writers is ever-increasing. So, what does it take to be a good technical writer? How is technical writing different than other forms of writing?

First of all, technical writers should know about the product they work with. If you know a lot about alternative energy, for example, you might want to write reports for a solar power company. Some companies simply need good writers, whether they know about the product or not. However, it's always best to be knowledgeable about a specific area.

But the most important quality of technical writing is *the ability to explain things to the beginner.* How many times have you tried to make sense of instruction manuals, only to find the wording impossible or the steps unclear? It's a frustrating experience! Now that technology is expanding so rapidly, manufacturers know the value of friendly, clear writing. This is where your writing skills pay off.

A good technical writer uses *conversational*, uncomplicated English. Remember, in this medium you're not trying to master a fancy style or find lovely words! The writing should be straightforward; it should sound like someone is right there explaining how to use the product. This might sound easy, but it's not!

Finally, the explanation has to unfold *step-by-step.* If you're explaining how to use a computer, for example, begin by demonstrating how to turn it on. You should also instruct the reader how to practice each step as it appears. This will give the person a sense of progress.

Assignment

A) Look through a published manual. Does it achieve the clarity that's needed for an effective manual? What kind of tone, if any, does the writer have?

Assignment

B) Write at least one page explaining how to use or make a product. You might want to explain how to play a computer game, or how to make a kite. Be sure to follow the tips given above.

Afterwards, give your paper to someone. Have her try to follow the instruction. Afterwards, get feedback; find out what was clear or unclear. This will give you some idea of what it takes to be a technical writer.

Travel Writing

Can you imagine being paid to travel and to write about the places you visit? Too good to be true? Well, believe it or not, the travel writer does just this. In a sense, he reviews travel destinations just as others review books or films.

There are different types of travel writing, each of which serves a specific purpose. If you were to write a *travel guide,* for example, you would provide vacationers with information about transportation, currency, restaurants, airports, hotels, places of interest, and so forth. These guides are very detailed, so you must know the location well. However, keep in mind that travel guides are not about *you.* They are about a place, so keep personal stories out of it.

Travel articles, which are less detailed than guides, are featured in the "travel section" of periodicals. People turn to these articles for news about vacation spots. These pieces highlight the pros and cons of travel destinations.

Sometimes travel writers publish book-length accounts of their journeys. These books are reflections of a writer who is *immersed* in a culture. Unlike the guide and the article, travel books vary in style and intention. Some feature the author's personal stories and observations. Maybe the author is returning to her place of birth, where she rediscovers her past; maybe she takes a pilgrimage to a sacred spot. Other books are more objective, excluding personal material.

Assignment

A) Review a travel article from a local periodical. Does it provide enough information? Does it inspire you to visit the location?

Assignment

B) Write a travel article about your favorite vacation spot or your home town. If you like, include photos. When you're done, present the article to your class. See if your classmates want to visit the location.

You will want to include the following information:

- **Transportation:** Provide facts about public transportation, taxi rates, railroads, boat travel, and airports.

- **Hotels:** List quality hotels in all price ranges, including youth hostels.

- **Places of Interest:** Include any well-known locations, both in and around the area. Try to highlight some lesser-known places.

- **Weather:** Let the traveler know what to expect from the seasonal weather.

- **Customs:** Inform the traveler about local propriety. This includes practical issues, such as tipping; but it also touches upon social customs. In some cultures, for example, wearing shorts might be offensive; in another, burping at the dinner table might be acceptable!

Writing a Greeting Card

We send cards for many occasions: birthdays, weddings, anniversaries, births, graduations, illnesses, deaths, and so forth. Cards also express our sentiments: longing, love, appreciation, and regret, to name a few. It's no wonder that greeting cards are big business!

Have you ever wondered who writes greeting cards? Who invents the sayings? What are the elements of a good greeting card?

Although many cards contain recycled sayings, such as "Get well soon" or "Happy birthday," novelty remains a key to success. Think about some of your favorite greeting cards—they probably all have some element of originality. "Here's wishing you the best birthday ever!" is dull compared to "This happens once every 365 days! Enjoy it NOW!"

Since the greeting card writer has limited space, he must be succinct. After all, the point of greeting cards is to *express direct sentiments. How* you present the idea is essential. So, what are some of the different approaches?

Short poems are popular, as are brief, quirky statements. Depending on the design of the card, you might want a question/answer format. If the front of the card says, "What's even better than graduating from college?" the inside should have a witty answer: "Nothing...it's all downhill from here!"

Of course, a greeting card writer must always be sensitive to the intent of the card. The passing of a loved one should not be met with humor, just as an anniversary card should be celebratory. In some cases, however, humor can be tastefully achieved by contrasting the mood of the occasion: "Get well soon...my tennis racket is rusting!"

Assignment

A) Choose three occasions or sentiments and create three greeting cards. Feel free to make a design. Share your cards with others. You might even want to send your ideas to a greeting card company.

The Dictionary Game

The Dictionary Game is a fun activity that provides laughs while teaching vocabulary. Here's how it works.

The teacher writes a word that no one in the class can define. Let's say she chooses the word 'avuncular.' Now, each student makes up a definition for 'avuncular.' The idea is to fool your classmates by writing a definition that sounds correct. Something like "one who runs around a lot" might be suitable. When you're done, fold your paper and hand it in to your teacher. The teacher, meanwhile, writes the real meaning of the word, which is mixed with all the false definitions.

Now comes the fun part. The teacher reads all the definitions out loud, and then people vote for the definition they think is correct. (You *cannot* vote for your own definition!) After the votes are tallied, the teacher reads the real definition. The person whose definition has the most votes is the winner, and gets to choose the next word.

By the way, 'avuncular' means "pertaining to an uncle."

How Many Words?

This is a very simple word game that requires at least two players, a word, and a timer. The game begins when a word is chosen. Let's say the group chooses the following word:

TREASURE

Now each player writes down words that use the letters in 'treasure.' Here are a few answers: *sure, tea, at, tear,* and *seat*. (One letter words don't count.) The list goes on. See if you can find some more.

Decide as a group on the time limit for finding words. When you're done, compare lists. Whoever made the most words is the winner.

Note: It's okay to "challenge" a player if you doubt the authenticity of a word. If the word can't be found in the dictionary, the person crosses that word off his list. However, if the word exists, and the player can define it, the challenger loses a word.

"Ghost"

"Ghost" is a fun word game for two people. The object of the game is *not* to spell a word! The rules are simple.

Have a piece of paper and a pencil ready. Flip a coin to see who goes first. Player 1 begins by writing any letter of the alphabet. Let's say she writes a T.

Next, her partner adds a letter. However, it has to be a letter that can eventually create a word. If he adds a K to the T, for example, the first person can say "challenge," in which case he would have to come up with a word that begins with TK! Instead, let's say he chooses O.

Now, even though TO makes a word, you have to spell a *three-letter word* in order to lose. So, player 1 must add another letter that won't spell a word. If she chooses P, for instance, she loses, having spelled TOP. Let's say she chooses R, which spells TOR.

Player 2 has the right to challenge or to add another letter. Say he chooses C, spelling TORC. Obviously, player 1 is in a difficult position. If she adds an H, she'll spell TORCH, but she can't think of any other words that begin TORC. At this point, she'll either give up or challenge. Whoever wins gets to go first next time.

"Ghost" is a fun game that will get you thinking about words, words, words! It's also a great game to play on long drives!

Spoonerisms!

We're all familiar with tongue-twisters, but few of us ever enter into the wonderful world of *spoonerisms!* You see, you can **talk in spoonerisms** if you **spalk in toonerisms**. You can tell the story of "Little Red Riding Hood," or "Rittle Led Hiding Rood."

Got it? Spoonerisms are made by exchanging the first consonants of words that are beside each other. "Very beautiful," becomes "Bery veautiful." Of course, talking in spoonerisms is not easy. If you've ever heard a skilled spoonerist, you know this. Before continuing on to our assignment, let's take a look at a normal sentence transformed into a spoonerism:

- Gerald was crying when he saw the wounded bird flying alone.
- Cerald was grying when he saw the bounded word flying alone.

Notice that we don't apply the spoonerism to small words. Also, notice that we didn't change the words "flying alone." This is because 'alone' begins with a vowel. However, skilled spoonerists might change it to "lying falone."

<u>Assignment</u>

A) We're going to take our first step into spoonerisms by *writing* them. Retell a famous fairy tale, like "Back and the Jeanstalk," in spoonerisms. Condense the story into one page.

When you're done, read it out loud many times. This will increase your ability to talk in spoonerisms. Once you've mastered that talent, you'll be the life of the party!

More Writing Assignments

The following is a list of twenty additional writing assignments and writing topics. Most of them introduce types of writing that will need explanation. As often as possible, you should find published models of the writing.

- Ghost writing

- Personification

- Screenplay

- Play writing

- Comic strip

- Foreign language words and expressions common in English

- Satire

- Prose poetry

- Concrete poetry

- Query letter

- Petition

- Melodrama

- Make up a historical document

- Childhood story

- Letter from prison

- Invent words and their definitions

- A dream

- Message in a bottle

- Last person left on Earth

- Message from the year 2500

Answer Key

Page 20, Colons and Semicolons

A)

1. project:
2. trouble;
3. These are my favorite dances:
4. dynamite;
5. voice; manner;
6. excited;
7. Danger; Monster;
8. ceremony:

B)

1. vegetarians;
2. following:
3. there;
4. companies:
5. Brando; Margret;
6. astronomy;
7. These are the finalists in the competition:
8. question:

Page 23, Parentheses and Dashes
(Answers may vary)

A)

1. Our annual visit to Lake Tahoe (it was the fourth year in a row) was terrific.
2. ...canceled—what a drag!
3. ... breathing—thank God she was a doctor!
4. Chewing tobacco is popular in these parts (about 35% of the people do it).
5. The quote you're looking for (page 73) is fascinating.
6. ...budget—we spent an extra 17 million dollars!
7. Lisa (my little sister) is coming to the family party.
8. ...accident—he was cheerful, lighthearted, and talkative.

B)

1. ...abruptly—how disappointing!
2. ...friend (she's from Texas)....
3. ...passage (page 198)....
4. ...warning—next time....

5. ...licorice (about 13 pieces, I think)....
6. Dragons (like the ones in Chinese mythology)....
7. ...Independence (1776)....
8. I'm sorry—I....

Page 28, Parallel Construction

A)

1. ...and envelopes.
2. ...and time of departure....
3. ...and the British.
4. ...in the cupboard....
5. ...the principal is well-liked.
6. ...and the drive was fun.
7. ...a hard-working student....
8. ...and spaciousness....

B)

1. ...or my height.
2. ...and a long tongue.
3. ...boredom....
4. ...she is liked....
5. ...summer.
6. ...and three tents.
7. ...and behind the door.
8. ...and antique gates.

Page 31, Modifiers
(Answers may vary)

A)

1. Bicycling home from school, we saw the ice cream truck.
2. He sold the old, broken car to the dump.
3. After my baby sister brushed her teeth for the first time, my mom gave her a kiss.
4. The world was changed after astronauts landed on the moon.
5. His business partner, Ralph, is a man who owns properties.
6. The fans cheered as the baseball hero swung the bat.
7. Camping on the mountain, Julian watched the meteor shower.
8. Leaving for Tennessee, she left her luggage in the taxi.

B)

1. We should think about putting the bookcase between the night stand and the dresser.
2. To join the rehearsals, you must have permission slips signed.
3. While running on the beach, he twisted his ankle trying a cartwheel.
4. Rowing across the lake in our canoe, we saw a frog.
5. In the middle of the night, it's handy to have a telescope.
6. After getting ready for the play, we couldn't open the curtain.
7. Upset by the bad weather, the officials canceled the tennis tournament.
8. Dreaming of a werewolf, I woke to the yapping of coyotes.

Page 35, Sentence Combining
(Answers may vary)

A)

1. Mrs. Reyes wrote an excellent play about her family.
2. To ensure a safe trip, a sailor should always be aware of weather conditions.
3. No one would talk to him because he was always bitter.
4. Janet, who is eighteen, attends Harvard college and wants to major in psychology.
5. The ancient volcano is about to erupt.
6. Bradly, who is tall and thin, likes to read and play guitar.
7. After we went to the diner, we went to the lake, where we like to swim at night.
8. Although he shouted, his stubborn dog wouldn't come.

B)

1. The salad, which has ripe avocado mixed in, is fresh from the garden.
2. Houdini was a great magician who could escape from chains.
3. There is grass on the mountaintop where the herd of elk lives.
4. After playing tennis, we went to school and met Jonathan.
5. Sherman, our neighbor's sweet cat, doesn't have a tail.
6. Although she wrote to the president, her letter was ignored.
7. For that recipe, you will need Indian spices, butter and salt.
8. The bookstore was closed because today is a holiday.